DEVIZES

history & guide

In *The History of the Worthies of England* published posthumously in 1662, Thomas Fuller described Wiltshire as 'a pleasant county and of great variety'. He continued: 'I have heard a wise man say that an ox left to himself would, of all England, choose to live in the north, a sheep in the south part hereof, and a man in the middle betwixt both, as partaking of the pleasure of the plain, and the wealth of the deep country.'

DEVIZES

history & guide

Lorna Haycock

TEMPUS

First published 1993
This edition 2000
Reprinted 2006

Tempus Publishing Ltd
The Mill, Brimscombe Port
Stroud, Gloucestershire GL5 2QG
www.tempus-publishing.com

British Library Cataloguing in Publication Data.
A catalogue record for this book is available from the British Library.

ISBN 0 7524 2159 X

Typesetting and origination by Tempus Publishing.
Printed in Great Britain

CONTENTS

Preface and Acknowledgements   6

1   Before Devizes   7

2   The Castle Satellite   10

3   The Medieval Town   18

4   The Sixteenth and Seventeenth Centuries:
     Urban and Commercial Growth   26

5   Men in Visors   35

6   Georgian Devizes: The Golden Age   44

7   Inns and Travel   58

8   The Nineteenth Century: The Age of Improvement   65

9   The Twentieth Century: Continuity and Change   80

     The Walking Tour   93

     The Next Steps   123

     Index   125

PREFACE & ACKNOWLEDGEMENTS

Since the first edition of this book was published in 1993, Devizes has grown in population and extent, and further changes are imminent in the town centre. Situated close to the edge of the Wiltshire Downs and the Vale of Pewsey, Devizes manages to combine the functions of a country market town with architectural distinction and despite encroaching traffic and the pace of modern life retains its character and a special charm. The town has much to fascinate residents and visitors, both in its visual appeal and in its colourful past. I trust that this new edition will stimulate respect for the architectural legacy of Devizes and for its rich heritage that has been handed down over a thousand years.

Many people have assisted in the preparation of this book by sharing with me information and photographs. I am conscious of my debt to them and to the many Devizes townspeople who have contributed to this story. I should particularly like to thank John Chandler, Kate Fielden, Paul Robinson and James Thomas for their advice. Barrie Barrett, Pamela Slocombe and Daphne Bryant gave me useful information on the Kennet and Avon Canal and Devizes buildings and inns. I am grateful to David Buxton, Barbara Fuller, Ian Leonard, Derek Parker, Dick and Mary Larden, Norman and Mona Ellis, Wadworth & Co. Ltd and Kennet District Council for access to their photographic collections and to Nick Griffiths for the use of his drawings.

CHAPTER 1

Before Devizes

Dr James Davis, in his *Origines Divisianae* in 1750 satirised the propensity of eighteenth-century antiquaries to ascribe an ancient origin to Devizes.

> 'As to your town, no doubt but it was ancient, ... but not quite so old as the Flood, Babel, Babylon or Rome. The inhabitants are not the worse for not having long pedigrees, or Roman blood in their veins; they may be contented with a Descent no earlier than the Normans'.

It is a curious fact that Devizes, situated in an area which is exceptionally rich in prehistoric remains, is a relatively modern creation. Lying in the centre of Wiltshire between the 'chalk' and the 'cheese' countries, Devizes is situated on a plateau of upper greensand on the western extremity of the Marlborough Downs, overlooking the Pewsey Vale to the east and the Avon Valley to the west. Its soil and geographical position gave the area fertility and defence, but its lack of running water was perhaps a deterrent to early settlement, as well as inhibiting later industrial development. Despite lying between the two great river systems of Wiltshire, flowing to Bournemouth and Bristol, water supply until 1877 came from wells sunk in the greensand.

Few traces of prehistoric settlement survive in the immediate vicinity of Devizes. Apart from a few flint flakes and scrapers discovered near Roundway and Etchilhampton, the most important finds from the Neolithic and Bronze Ages are a polished stone axe from Old Park and a tanged and barbed arrowhead from Pans Lane. The Bronze Age barrows within the hill fort on Roundway Down contained artefacts and skeletons, but there is a general dearth of Iron Age finds, which casts doubt on the theory that there was a hill fort on the site of the present castle. There are certainly more traces of Roman activity in the district, though not of a Roman military presence, despite the building of a Roman road across the downs from Mildenhall to Sandy Lane a few miles away.

Aerial photography has revealed the foundations of a Roman villa at Mother Anthony's Well at the foot of Roundway Down and

Eight of the Roman bronze images of household gods and Celtic deities found on the Green in 1699 and now in the British Museum.

the excavation of skeletons and artefacts to the east and south of Devizes suggests that there was a small Romano-British settlement or religious site in the Southbroom and Wick areas. In 1699 a blue earthen pot containing several hundred bronze Imperial coins was found on the Green, where fifteen years later twenty-one Penates, miniature images of household gods and Celtic deities, were also discovered; eight of them survive today in the British Museum. These miniatures aroused such interest that they were engraved on an early-eighteenth century map of the counties of Wiltshire, Hampshire and Dorset and were exhibited around the country. In 1724, William Stukeley reported that Roman antiquities were being 'found here every day'.

During the cutting of the Berks and Hants Extension Railway in 1861, a skeleton, some high quality Samian and blackware pottery, an axe head and iron knives were discovered and another skeleton was found when Pans Lane Halt was being constructed in 1929. The excavation of a small Romano-British cemetery on the site of Southbroom Junior School and the existence of many third- and fourth-century Imperial coins and pottery sherds in the Nursteed Road and Pans Lane areas indicate that that there must have been a settlement nearby which was occupied for some considerable time. Recent excavations at Roundway Hospital have also uncovered Roman votive material in the form of fishes, while the Wayside Farm development has revealed skeletons, pottery, ironwork, corn ovens, animal bones and coins from a Romano-British farmstead which existed in the fourth and fifth centuries. There seems, too, to have been some sort of temple or shrine nearby, where rituals were performed.

A Saxon presence is more elusive. Excavations on Roundway Down in 1840 uncovered a female skeleton, facing east to west and therefore probably a Christian burial, dating from the seventh century. She was evidently a woman of some status, for around her

neck were several garnets set in gold, and nearby lay two pins fastened with a gold chain. No Saxon artefacts have been found in Devizes itself, however, although it was surrounded by Saxon settlements at Potterne, Lavington and Cannings. Perhaps the prestige of the community at Potterne two miles away, with an important pre-conquest church and baptistery, attracted settlement away from Devizes. The town is not mentioned in Domesday Book, and it was not until the late eleventh century that a community of any size began to develop as a satellite to the Norman castle.

Roman pottery found on the outskirts of Devizes, now in Devizes Museum.

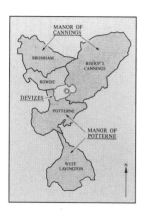

Ad Divisas.

CHAPTER 2

The Castle Satellite

It is appropriate that a castle is the centre piece of the coat of arms of Devizes, for to the castle the town owes its name, existence and early history. The first Devizes castle was constructed around 1080 by Osmund, Bishop of Salisbury, who later also completed the cathedral at Old Sarum. His castle, built on the boundaries of his manors of Potterne and Cannings with the King's manor of Rowde, became known as *castrum ad divisas*, the castle at the boundaries. It was constructed on a naturally defensive site, a spur of land with three sloping sides that only needed some form of barrier across the neck of this promontory to make it impregnable. Osmund's castle was probably a wooden motte and bailey castle, with a three-storey tower on a palisaded mound. The outer bailey, defended by a ditch, stockade and drawbridge, contained stores, stables and soldiers' quarters. Because of its strategic position it was used to house state prisoners, the most illustrious of whom was Robert, Duke of Normandy, the Conqueror's eldest son, imprisoned there for twenty years following defeat in a power struggle with his younger brother, Henry I. As happened with so many of these early wooden structures the castle was burnt down, this one in 1113; its rebuilding in stone was the work of Osmund's successor as Bishop of Salisbury, Roger of Caen.

From humble beginnings as an obscure priest in Normandy, Roger was discovered by Henry I on one of his continental campaigns to be remarkably swift at saying the mass and was immediately engaged as royal chaplain. Roger's abilities and ambition ensured his rapid promotion to the posts of Bishop of Salisbury and Justiciar of England. He deputized for Henry when the king was abroad, being known as Procurator or Viceroy. More a secular baron than a spiritual leader, he strengthened his hold on power by promoting his son to be Chancellor and two of his nephews (one of whom was also Treasurer) to bishoprics. To defend his lands he built or rebuilt a string of castles at Malmesbury, Sherborne and Devizes, also acquiring the royal castle at Old Sarum and enlarging the cathedral there.

The Borough Arms on an old painted panel in the Town Hall.

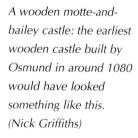

A wooden motte-and-bailey castle: the earliest wooden castle built by Osmund in around 1080 would have looked something like this. (Nick Griffiths)

Roger's castle at Devizes was described by contemporary chroniclers as 'the finest and most splendid in Europe' and 'a noble castle strongly defended by Art and Nature'. Very few traces of this building now remain, though parts of the foundations of the original keep were uncovered during the construction of the nineteenth-century castle. But, judging from the evidence of surviving contemporary castles such as Rochester, built by Roger's friend, the Archbishop of Canterbury, it probably had a massive square keep, inner and outer baileys defended by battlemented walls with towers at the angles, a gateway with portcullises and a very deep moat with vertical sides. Stone for building the castle may have come from Hazelbury, Box. John Leland visited the ruined castle in 1545, describing it as:

'… stately avauncyd upon an high ground, defendyd partly by nature with dykes, the yere [earth] whereof is cast up a slope, and that of a great height to defence of the waulle. The kepe or dungeon of it set upon an hille – is a peace of muche goodly buylding – There remayne dyvers goodly towers yet in the outer waull of the castle – the principall gate that ledithe in to the towne is yet of a great strength, and hath places for seven or eight portcullises.'

A report on the castle in 1610 by topographer John Norden listed 'five very high decayed towers, two decayed chapels and a large ruined hall standing within the keep upon a most lofty artificial mound'. The hall within the keep contained residential apartments while the dungeons were on the lower storey.

Medieval documents mention other rooms and buildings within the 10-acre complex, such as wardrobe, nursery, larder, tailor's chamber, pantry, bake-house, granary and aviary.

The entrance to the castle was through the present Castle Lane next to the Bear Hotel where there was a gatehouse or barbican, containing a prison and a drawbridge. Leading to this was the stockaded, raised approach of the *Bretasche* or Brittox, with a wooden barbican containing a prison; a 1551 lease refers to 'The Brode Gate with a cottage adjoining called the Cage'. The Brittox, however, is badly aligned with Castle Lane. An eighteenth-century rent book mentions a gatehouse in Short Street, which would have led more directly towards the main gate and may have been part of a line of outer defensive entrances. When the railway tunnel was being dug under the castle mound in 1861, engineers discovered that the moat was much deeper than originally thought, at least 45ft lower than the present level. Hillworth Road leading to Gallows Ditch is on the summit of the outer bank of the earthworks. During the construction of the Corn Exchange in 1857, the castle ditch across the neck of the promontory on which the castle was built was found to be about 20ft deep with steep sides. The judgement of the writer of *Gesta Stephani* in 1140 that 'the fortifications were splendid and impregnable' seems therefore fully justified.

A conjectural view of Devizes' medieval stone castle, from a painting by James Waylen.

The years 1139 to 1141, the period of civil war between Stephen and Matilda, were perhaps the most eventful time in the history of Devizes castle. Henry I had spent his last years trying to secure the succession for Matilda, his only child after his son was drowned in 1119. The barons and bishops, including Roger, were persuaded to swear to accept her as Queen. But when Henry died in 1135 his nephew, Stephen of Blois, invaded England to claim the throne. He was supported by many nobles and bishops, who perhaps thought that Stephen was more pliable than Matilda, though they claimed to be absolved from their oath to recognize her because Henry had married her to a foreigner, the Count of Anjou, without their consent. Stephen, apprehensive of an attack from Matilda's supporters, summoned a council at Oxford. A dispute over accommodation between Stephen's French favourites and Roger's retainers developed into a fracas which Stephen used as an excuse to arrest his over-mighty subject Roger, his son and two of his nephews. One nephew, however, escaped to join Matilda of Ramsbury, Roger's mistress, in Devizes castle. Stephen rode to Devizes, taking Roger and his son as hostages, and had a gibbet erected in front of the castle gate, where he paraded young Roger with a rope around his neck. Within three days Matilda of Ramsbury surrendered the castle to save her son's life. Bishop Roger was released from the cowshed in which he had been locked, and was forced to surrender his lands and possessions to Stephen, including the plate, jewels and 40,000 marks (or £26,667 13s 4d) found in the castle.

During the west country campaigns between Matilda's followers and Stephen's supporters, Devizes castle saw much action, its strength and strategic position making it a tempting prize in this increasingly anarchical period. Robert Fitzhubert, a Flemish adventurer, boasted that if he possessed Devizes castle he could keep in subjection all the lands between London and the west. He captured the castle on a stormy night, using leather ladders to avoid waking the garrison, and laid waste the surrounding countryside. But he too was captured and paraded in front of the castle to force the garrison to surrender; when they refused, he and two of his nephews were hanged on the site of the present market place. Stephen, however, bribed the garrison to hand over the castle, which he gave to his son-in-law, Count Hervey of Brittany.

A small town was by this time developing outside the castle's outer bailey, as traders and craftsmen set up their stalls and booths to provide the castle garrison with goods and services. Thoroughly alienated by the pillaging and ravages of Fitzhubert and other freebooters, the 'simple rustics' besieged the castle and forced Hervey to surrender it to Matilda's forces. By now Matilda had secured the royal treasure and had been proclaimed Queen. To reward the townspeople for their support in winning back the castle she awarded them a charter in 1141, granting them freedom from certain tolls: 'My burgesses of Devizes, in consideration of their service, are exempt from land-toll, ferry-toll, fair-toll and every other Custom throughout the whole realm and the seaports.' In practice this meant the privilege of holding a market. During these years Matilda was often in Devizes, holding several councils in the castle and issuing thirteen of her known charters here. In 1141, pursued by Stephen's forces, she rode the forty miles from Winchester to Devizes, sitting astride like a man for greater speed, and arriving 'more dead than alive' in the words of a chronicler. She was sent on to safety at Gloucester bound in a litter. Matilda's son, Henry, used Devizes as the base for his west country campaigns and forced Stephen to recognize him as heir to the throne. Devizes castle remained in the hands of the Crown until the seventeenth century. The lordship of the castle was one of the most important grants in the gift of the Crown, encompassing an area including Devizes and Rowde, the Old and New Parks, the right of appointment to the two churches and the forests of Chippenham and Melksham.

The castle continued to be used as a prison and a treasury. In 1209 King John's second wife, Isabella, imprisoned in Devizes since 1206, gave birth to a son in the castle, and in 1216 King John sent the Crown jewels and royal regalia there for safety during the French invasion. It was obviously a secure stronghold. In the thirteenth and fourteenth centuries there are many records of payments to carpenters, stonemasons and labourers for repair work and for the procurement of Corsham slates, Hazelbury stone and wood from the Royal forests. This must have provided much local employment.

During Henry III's reign another distinguished political figure was imprisoned in Devizes castle. The King's French courtiers, jealous of the power of Hubert de Burgh, Earl of Kent and Justiciar of the realm, who had defeated the French fleet in the baronial wars, persuaded Henry to dismiss him and imprison him in Devizes castle in 1232. He was put in chains and guarded by four earls and four knights, but hearing that his enemy, Peter des Roches, was plotting to have him killed, Hubert persuaded two of his warders to help him escape. Still fettered, he was carried on the shoulders of one of them down the steep bank of the inner bailey and across the

The rescue of Hubert de Burgh from St John's church in 1232: an impression by James Waylen.

ditch to seek sanctuary in nearby St John's church. He was soon recaptured and returned to the castle, where he was kept in solitary confinement in three pairs of iron fetters. The violation of the right of sanctuary had, however, offended the church authorities; the Bishop of Salisbury excommunicated the castle garrison and demanded that de Burgh be returned to the church. The King then secretly ordered the county sheriff to surround and fence the churchyard to prevent his escape from St John's, but a party of the King's opponents broke down the fence and carried Hubert off to Wales.

The castle was defended by knights who held nearby Crown lands in return for forty days military service in time of war or financial payments in peacetime. In Henry III's reign, for example, the vineyards at Stert were held for 8s 4d a year. These payments in lieu of military service continued long after the castle ceased to exist as a royal fortress. In 1722 they were still payable at Michaelmas under the name of castle ground rents. On Edward I's marriage to Margaret of France in 1299, Devizes castle and town became part of her marriage settlement. From henceforth it was the queen who appointed the constables of the castle and took the rents from the lands. Members of the royal family were frequent visitors to Devizes. Orders survive for the carriage of wine from Southampton to Devizes in 1302 'against the King's arrival there'. King John left Prince Henry, the future Henry III, in the care of the castle governor, and Edward I used to spend his Easters hawking and hunting in the castle parks. In 1216 thirty falcons, thirty greyhounds, thirty grooms and thirty horses had been provided for the Royal chase.

Bishop Roger had created Old Park, a thickly wooded deer park of about 600 acres, bounded by a 15ft-wide rampart to protect his sport. The line of the old bank, known as the Deer's Leap, is still visible to the right of the track to Whistley beyond Hartmoor. The boundary then crosses the valley past Lower Park Farm to Sunnyside Farm, and follows the present Bath road and canal towpath. In the centre of the park was a keeper's lodge, surrounded by a 3ft-deep moat made by two streams that met there. Stag horns were later found in this moat when the house was pulled down in 1830. The present Hartmoor Road and its continuing lane constituted the main route between the castle and the Bishop of Salisbury's possessions at Potterne, Estcroft Hill being the natural exit from the castle leading to this road along the deer park boundary. Until the mid-eighteenth century Hartmoor Road was the main thoroughfare to Potterne, and was in use as a coach road leading to Five Lanes. It was known as the Devizes Sand Way. The pasture land of the New Park, first recorded in 1157, was probably also surrounded by a bank and ditch. It encompassed the present Roundway Park area and was approached through the Keeper's Walk, later corrupted to Quakers' Walk. The teeming wildlife of the Devizes parks provided food, not only for the Royal household at Westminster, but also for local poachers who often found themselves detained in the castle, which was well supplied with iron chains and manacles to maintain its dominance over the local community.

CHAPTER 3

The Medieval Town

Like Richmond in Yorkshire and Launceston in Cornwall, Devizes is a classic example of a town which grew up as an urban satellite to a castle. The size and design of the concentric ditches of the town and castle and the neatly laid out 32ft-wide burgage plots in New Park Street and the Market Place suggest that this was a deliberately planned town rather than a haphazard and spontaneous development. A large number of workers would have been needed to construct such a mighty castle, and traders and craftsmen would be encouraged to supply its material needs. Excavations in New Park Street in 1986 and 1987 uncovered evidence for habitation in the form of cess pits dating from the late twelfth century and also revealed the line of the outer defences of the medieval town underneath or on the north-east side of Commercial Road.

Although a market was first recorded in 1228, it must have already existed for many years. The present market place was then the outer bailey of the castle; the early medieval market place was in the wide space outside St Mary's church, which was then not restricted by the later in-filling by buildings in Maryport Street and Monday Market Street. A market cross stood at the corner of the present White Bear, where the corn market was held and the cattle market took place westward of St Mary's church. The trading community of Devizes had become so important by 1295 that it was summoned to send two representatives to Edward I's Model Parliament, and continued to be represented in most of the other medieval parliaments. The town, however, seems to have suffered a period of economic decline between 1332 and 1362 and was not then represented in the House of Commons. This recession is reflected in the tax ranking of Devizes. In the 1332 tax of a tenth on moveable property, Devizes had thirty eight taxpayers, with three traders each contributing more than 10s of the borough's total assessment of 115s; the town ranked sixth in the county. But in 1334 it was not in the top forty-two in Wiltshire and lagged behind places such as Steeple Ashton and All Cannings.

Devizes traders were fiercely protective of their market. After an enquiry in Henry III's reign, it was decreed that no market should

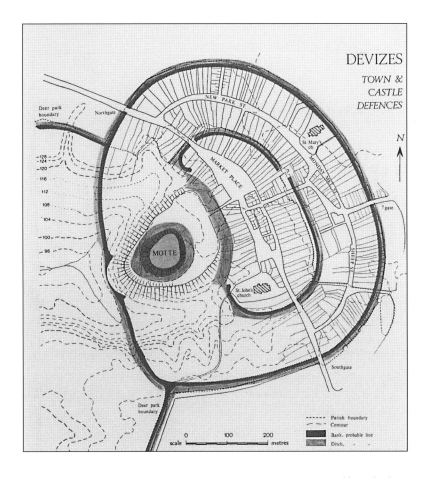

The medieval street plan of Devizes showing the positions of the original banks and ditches.

be held within seven miles of the borough. It was alleged that Richard de Rokell, a Crown tenant, had held a market at Market Lavington on the day preceding Devizes market, with the result that receipts from Devizes market had fallen from £16 to £12. This case accounts for the subsequent decline of Market Lavington as a commercial centre and also establishes the fact that a market was already being held at Devizes on Thursdays. The Devizes burgesses evidently felt sufficiently self-confident to also complain that the Earl of Warwick and Philip Bassett, late constables of the castle, had established stalls in the market at reduced rents to the detriment of their own profits. The grant of a Merchant Guild by Edward III in 1377 assisted this growing sense of mutual protection. The Devizes Guild was the only one in Wiltshire to bear arms, a privilege confirmed by the Heralds' visitations in 1565 and 1623.

The early traders were mostly connected with the leather industry, the tanners, skinners, glovers and cordwainers. Edmund le Glover appears in a deed of 1302 and Walter le Glover in 1309. A tannery is mentioned in 1371 and the tanners' market was held in front of St John's Alley. There was also a metal trade of some

An aerial view of Devizes showing how the street pattern developed around the castle. This 1960s photograph shows the castle (top left) and the railway station (left of top centre), closed in 1966.

importance; a brazier is listed in 1379, and the iron ore was probably smelted in Old Park. But during the course of the fourteenth century the cloth trade gradually became more important with the general switch in England from exporting raw wool, heavily taxed to finance Edward III's wars against France, to the production of finished cloth. A dyer is noted in the town as early as 1281. By 1315 Devizes merchants were already exporting cloth of Ghent to the French town of St Omer, where English merchants had their staple. The interruption of foreign imports during the Hundred Years War assisted the further expansion of the woollen trade. There was evidently a considerable commerce in white broadcloth or 'Vize blankets', first mentioned in 1429. William Page, a Devizes clothier at the end of the fifteenth century, once disposed of £100 worth of cloth in a single deal. Fourteenth-century documents refer regularly to craftsmen connected with the woollen trade, such as John le Webbe, Richard Cardmaker and William Smyth, a clothier who became so wealthy that he was able to finance the rebuilding of the nave of St Mary's church.

Great Porch House in Monday Market Street.

If the castle had spawned the growth of Devizes as a commercial town, paradoxically the decline of the castle's military importance in the fourteenth century also helped in the community's continued expansion and industrial development. Several enquiries in the fourteenth century revealed that the outer bailey walls had been breached and that much building material had been taken away as 'any man is able to go into the castle there'. It was obviously no longer being kept in a defensible state. A mansion had been built in the inner bailey as a more comfortable residence and in the reign of Henry VII the keep was demolished. In 1526, material was taken from the castle to build old Bromham House. It was possible therefore for the townsmen to encroach on the large open space of the outer bailey and establish houses and shops there. The area became known as the New Port, first mentioned in 1309, the former market place being called the Old Port, and these

No. 4 St John's Court, a medieval hall house.

St Mary's church.

territories became conterminous with the two parishes of St John and St Mary. A new street was laid out between the north and south gates of the town, encompassing Northgate Street, the Market Place and Long Street. In 1411 a stall was granted in 'the New Port where the fish is sold'. From the early fourteenth century, houses and shops were being built on the Brittox, the stockaded path to the castle. William Coventry leased a shop, garret and cellar in the Brittox to a tenant in 1420; the shop was open to the street, with living quarters over and with stores in the cellar.

The medieval street pattern of Devizes which has survived intact, apart from the making of New Street (Snuff Street) in the early eighteenth century, the cutting of Station Road in the nineteenth century and the construction of the link road between New Park Street and Gains Lane, has been described as one of the most remarkable of any Norman town in the country. The dominant features of the ditches and defences of the castle have dictated the concentric layout of the town and the arrangement of the building plots in the town centre, which use the ditches as their boundaries.

Most of the early shops and houses were timber-framed with wattle and daub in-fill and thatched roofs. Few have survived, but in both the Old Port and the New Port it is possible to see examples of late medieval and Tudor dwellings. Great Porch House in Monday Market Street, probably built in the mid-fifteenth century, was originally a long single-storey hall with a gabled two-storey cross wing. A louvre in the roof shows that it had a hearth in the middle of the floor. The carved wooden corbels and the

A drawing showing the appearance of St John's church in its original form.

floral wall paintings at each end of the inside of the roof indicate that it was the home of a wealthy merchant. In the seventeenth century, an upper floor was inserted, and two centuries later the house was refaced in brick and given sash windows. Excavations nearby in 1938, 1990 and 1991 uncovered the foundations of another fifteenth-century house and a chalk-lined well. Number 4 St John's Court was the home of a Mayor of Devizes, Thomas Coventry, who died in 1451. Partially rebuilt in stone in the seventeenth century, it was re-fronted in 1842, using some stone from the repair of St John's church, but originally it would have been a single-storey timber hall 18ft by 15ft open to the roof. The houses in St John's Alley are slightly later, early-sixteenth century to mid-seventeenth century. They are timber-framed with brick and plaster in-filling, with overhanging jetties and curved beam ends. Until 1832, St John's Alley ran through into Wine Street and was formerly called Wine Street Alley.

The other significant medieval legacies are the churches of St John and St Mary. It is unusual for a small town to possess two churches of Norman foundation that retain so much of their original workmanship. It has always been thought that St John's church was built for the castle garrison about 1150 and that St Mary's church was constructed for the townspeople later. But it is clear that there was at least one chapel within the castle precincts that was probably more convenient for the garrison to use, and late-nineteenth-century excavations revealed the foundations of an earlier simpler church in St Mary's churchyard. It seems likely therefore that, as the town grew, the smaller St

St Mary's church: Norman chancel and Perpendicular nave with beam oak roof.

The chancel of St John's church, with restored Norman window, wall arcading, chancel arch and quadripartite roof.

Mary's church was pulled down and a new one built around 1150. Some ten years later the church of St John's was built to provide for the increasing castle personnel and to match the grandeur of the town church.

Both churches retain their vaulted Norman chancels and round-arched interior arcading, and both were enlarged and altered in Perpendicular style during the town's prosperous period in the fifteenth century. St John's has some of the finest Norman work in the county, apart perhaps from Malmesbury Abbey, and was described by John Britton in 1809 as 'one of the most interesting parochial churches in Britain'. Its Norman tower is rectangular, not square, and is supported on two semi-circular and two pointed arches, an unusual and interesting example of the Norman Transitional period of the twelfth century. The Norman work in the chancel is original except for the intersecting arcade on the east and south walls of the Sanctuary and the small window in the east wall. Much of this arcading was plastered over and hidden until the nineteenth-century restoration, but originally the triple arcading and semi-circular headed windows in the tower would have been visible from below before the fifteenth-century insertion of a ringing floor. The overall effect of the chancel, with its arcading, fish scale work and chevron moulding is astoundingly beautiful. Arthur Mee wrote, 'On any day it is splendid, but at night, floodlit, it is of surpassing loveliness'. St Mary's has similar arcading and chevron moulding, though the five Norman chancel windows were later replaced by a three-light Perpendicular window. The outer porch is Transitional Norman of around 1200 and the thick east wall of the north aisle and the west wall of the nave are also Norman.

In the fifteenth century, the nave of St John's was rebuilt in Perpendicular style, and north and south aisles and two entrance porches were added. The Lamb and Beauchamp chapels also date from this period. The nave, aisles and tower of St Mary's were rebuilt through the generosity of clothier William Smyth, who died in 1436, and is commemorated by a carved inscription on the nave roof, 'Pray for the soul of William Smyth who caused this church to be built'. St Mary's has the crocketed pinnacles, embattled parapets and gargoyles typical of the Perpendicular style. In this church, great stress seems to have been laid on visual effect, possibly because the worshippers were less sophisticated. Later alterations have revealed traces of wall frescoes and a possible Doom painting above the chancel arch; there are also several niches for statues of the Virgin Mary, and carvings on the nave roof corbels.

Devizes may have lost its medieval castle, but the two Norman churches and surviving domestic buildings attest to the solid base and growing status of the medieval town.

An inscription on St Mary's nave roof that commemorates William Smyth, a wealthy clothier who died in 1436.

CHAPTER 4

The Sixteenth and Seventeenth Centuries: Urban and Commercial Growth

It was in the sixteenth and seventeenth centuries that Devizes began to establish its own identity, free now from the control of the castle. The Tudors relied heavily on boroughs and parishes to administer local government, and the burgesses of Devizes found themselves responsible for a wide range of duties, supervising trade, registering apprentices, administering poor relief, charities and highways and preserving law and order. The mayor, first recorded in 1302, came to replace the constable of the castle as the leading figure in the town. He was chosen by the Common Council of around fifty, from the twelve or Capital Burgesses, though the number fluctuated. They were also elected by the Common Council, but this was as far as democracy went, for the councillors, usually local tradesmen, were chosen by co-option and the Corporation became a self-perpetuating oligarchy. The Council also appointed the borough officers, such as the town clerk, bailiffs, constables, chamberlains, searchers of leather and the ale taster and beadle. On special occasions the Capital Burgesses were expected to provide themselves with caps and gowns, but the Inferior Burgesses just had to wear 'a decent cloake of some sadd [dark] colour'.

The mayor enjoyed a great deal of prestige. He was given an entertainment allowance for a feast on the day after his inauguration and also had a special seat reserved for him in both churches; in St Mary's this was elaborately draped with a green cloth. Some mayors and councillors could not sign their names, but the rigour of Council meetings was alleviated for the burgesses by sack, burnt wine and sugar, and, on special occasions, by simnel cakes. In the early seventeenth century, greater efficiency was brought to the work of the Council by John Kent, a vigorous and well-educated town clerk, who also held the offices of mayor and borough MP at various times, and who caused to be written, for the sum of £6, the splendid illuminated Book of Constitutions of the

Borough, a copy of which is now in the library of the Wiltshire Archaeological and Natural History Society. The bald comment in the borough records that 'the work of the Town Clerk is much increased of late yeres' hides a wealth of meaning. This form of local government was officially recognized by the Royal charters of 1605 and 1639 and remained unchanged until the Municipal Corporations Act of 1835.

A large part of the town's revenue came from the profits of fairs and markets granted to the borough by the Crown in the sixteenth century. John Leland in 1545 described the market as 'very

Title page of John Kent's Book of Constitutions, 1628, now in the Wiltshire Archaeological Society's library.

A.D. 1630. 6TH CHARLES I.

JOHN KENT ESQ, AND WIFE.

S^T JOHN'S CHURCH, DEVIZES.

Brasses of John and Mary Kent in the Beauchamp chapel, St John's church.

*The Wool Hall,
forerunner of the present
Town Hall, with an
open ground-floor
cheese market. A detail
from Dore's map of
Devizes, 1759.*

celebrate'. The burgesses allocated pitches and collected tolls through the bailiffs; outsiders were only allowed after local traders were accommodated. James I's charter of 1605 prohibited strangers from exhibiting merchandise other than corn, victuals, cattle, wool or yarn of their own making except in gross or at the fairs. For all stalls, pitches and sacks of corn, tolls were taken at the Tolsey House, under the Guildhall in Wine Street, and goods had to be weighed at the common beams. Butchers were forbidden to sell meat in their own shops on Mondays and Thursdays so that they would be forced to go to the butchers' Shambles, at various times situated under the Guildhall, in the market-place or opposite St Mary's church in Short Street, which for a time was known as Butchers' Street. In 1574 there were twenty butchers selling meat in the market, but only the official town chandler could sell candles made from butchers' tallow. The Corporation fixed the prices of bread and ale; bread was sold in penny or halfpenny loaves, and in 1559 the maximum permitted price for a quart of best ale was a penny. Lime trees sheltered the Butter, Cheese, Yarn and Corn Crosses, at the south end of the market place and in Wine Street, though the Yarn Cross was replaced by a Yarn Hall in 1575 on the site of the present Town Hall. The tanners' standings were nearby in St John's Street, alongside the fishmongers and shoemakers, while hosiers and greengrocers had their stalls in High Street and poulterers in Wine Street. Devizes seems to have been renowned not only for its cattle, corn and wool markets but also for its fish. In the late seventeenth century John Aubrey described the market as 'a very plentiful market of everything but the best for fish in the county. They bring the fish from Poole hither.' Day labourers could also be hired in the market; by a ruling of 1560 they were to wait there for employment between the hours of 6 and 7 a.m. in the winter and 5 and 6 a.m. in the summer.

Various improvements were made to the market in the early seventeenth century, perhaps under the influence of John Kent. New wooden Shambles were erected in 1600, and in 1615 a Measuring House for corn was built on the site of the present market cross. In the same year the Yarn Hall was rebuilt as the Wool Hall, described by Celia Fiennes in the 1680s as 'a very good Market House set on stone pillars'. The increasingly profitable cheese market was held on the lower floor in the late seventeenth century, a tradition continued when the present Town Hall was built. The hall also accommodated the County Sessions, previously held under temporary hustings. The Merchant Guild, too, played an important part supervising trade in the borough. Originally it was headed by the mayor and met in the Guildhall, on the southwest corner of Wine Street, which by the late seventeenth century was adorned with a clock, a market bell and a gilded globe and fish on its turret. The Guild was reorganized in 1614 into three companies, the Drapers, Mercers and Leather sellers, who settled disputes among their members and protected their traders from outside competition. Each company had its own master and officers. The Drapers held quarterly meetings in the Weavers Hall, on the northern side of Wine Street. They used the upper storey only, the lower floor being let as shops, but the premises extended behind the present Barclays Bank with a great hall and buttery. The hall floor was originally strewn with rushes, though by 1700 the Drapers possessed a carpet worth £4. They used the nearby Antelope at the opposite corner of the Little Brittox for socializing. These companies supervised the training of apprentices and their admission as freemen on payment of 3s 4d when they received a certificate from the mayor. An apprentice, whose parents had to

Badges of the Devizes guilds, weavers on the left and tailors on the right. This painted panel hangs in the Town Hall.

pay a premium for his training, served for seven years and was subject to strict regulations; he was not to haunt alehouses, nor play cards or dice, nor 'commit fornication or contract himself in marriage'.

In his *Worthies of England* Thomas Fuller described Devizes as 'the best and biggest town for tradeing ... in this shire'. Although tanning, brewing and malting were still of considerable importance, it was the cloth trade which showed the most rapid growth in the sixteenth and seventeenth centuries. According to John Leland Devizes was 'most occupied by clothiers'. During the reign of Henry VIII, white wool cloth was sent from Devizes to London, Bristol and Southampton for export to Germany and Italy. A coarser cloth, serge, was woven in quantity in the seventeenth century; it was cheaper to produce as it was made from lower grade wool and found a ready local market, as well as later being exported as far afield as Muscovy. There was a dye house in the town by 1549, and increasing reference is made in local records to fullers, shearmen, cardmakers and weavers. Many clothiers became wealthy and influential in the government of the town. Richard Batt, three times mayor, was rated in the 1545 subsidy higher than the famous Malmesbury clothier, William Stumpe. Philip Coleman, a mercer, who died in 1700, possessed goods worth £1,404 and many different sorts of cloth, including East Indian silks and 'Norridge and Spittlefield stufs'. Henry Morris, after whom Morris Lane is named, owned two broad looms, and evidently conducted his extensive transactions on credit; in his will in 1572, he bequeathed to his cousin 'all my bille of debtes at London' and reserved some silver spoons 'for pawnes'. Although the civil war in the mid-seventeenth century temporarily disrupted the sale of wool and yarn, by the time Celia Fiennes visited the town in the 1680s, she could describe it as 'a very rich tradeing place for the clothing trade'.

Surviving wills provide a glimpse into the homes and lives of these sixteenth- and seventeenth-century Devizes traders, as do the inventories required for probate purposes in the church courts. Furniture and equipment were sparse and basic, consisting of feather or tester beds with curtains and valances, presses or wardrobes, chests of drawers, iron spits and jacks for cooking, pewter plates, warming pans and chamber pots. But there are also significant references to prized possessions, such as silver candlesticks, looking glasses, a gown trimmed with black fur, a salt box, coffee pot or a clock. Matthew Figgins, who died in 1708, had a 'mappe of the Worlde', five Caesar's heads and a picture of the

Inventory of the goods of Phillip Coleman, mercer, 1700.

Queen's arms, while surgeon Edward Anne, who died in 1687, left three pairs of organs, two pairs of virginals and one chest of viols, valued at £100 in all. These testamentary details are also valuable evidence for trade stock and tools. In 1669 Richard Bennett, a cutler, left three boxes of muster pikes and sword belts, ten boxes of knives and thirteen small elephants' teeth, valued at £13, presumably to be used for knife handles. The stock of Grave Morris, apothecary and former mayor of the town, included a marble grinding trough, rhubarb, senna, liquorice, cloves, cinnamon and quicksilver. Richard Harman, a grocer, sold writing paper, powdered ginger, soap, hat brushes, pins, tapes and lace, and also possessed a tobacco press to provide for the growing demand from pipe smokers. Other trades represented in the town include tilers, barbers, masons, haberdashers and jerkin makers, as well as a dentist or 'tothe drawer'.

The streets in which these houses and shops were situated were narrow and dirty, with jutting-out buildings, overhanging storeys and water spouts gushing rainwater into the road. Houses were still made of timber and plaster with thatched roofs. The development of Old Swan Yard in 1990 revealed sixteenth- and seventeenth-century timber framing in-filled with wattle hurdles and daub. In

1655, however, the Corporation ordered that all new houses were to be tiled, not thatched because of the fire risk. Fire-fighting equipment was rudimentary, consisting of buckets, ladders and fire hooks. There were many elm trees growing outside houses, and there was a horse pool in the market place near the entrance to the present Station Road, as well as at the end of Morris Lane in Sheep Street and at Chapel Corner near the Job Centre. Livestock evidently roamed the streets, as there was a pig pound on the wasteland on the Green, and in 1623 fines were imposed for retrieving wandering pigs, geese, ducks and turkeys. Frequent reference is made in late seventeenth-century records to 'Youstice', who seems to have been the town handyman, called upon to clean the streets and do odd jobs. A public lavatory, called 'the House of Office', existed; in 1634 it was taken down, the ground underneath filled with sand and a dwelling house erected over it. The streets were patrolled between 11 p.m. and 4 a.m. by a bellman, who was charged with admonishing residents to take care of their candles, fires and locks; he had power to summon the aid of the inhabitants in case of fire, and to make 'suspicious loiterers' go home.

The Borough Court, held on Fridays once a month, dealt with minor offences, such as theft, vagrancy, trespass, immorality and abusive language. Punishments were usually carried out in the market place. They included whipping at the old market and whipping cross, a stone pillar with a ball and cross on top, sitting in the stocks or being nailed to the pillory. In 1577 William Eyles was put in the stocks for the night for 'being rude to the mayor', while in 1659 James Reynolds was whipped for stealing two chamber pots. William Gamble, junior, was imprisoned for fighting with the watchman and 'breaking Thomas Smyth's head'; he was ordered to make satisfaction for the 'bludshed'. Cases of bigamy, vagrancy and boundary disputes are recorded in the borough archives, interspersed with more serious crimes, such as shoemaker John Clott putting rat poison in his wife's ale. In 1579 a Bridewell was built in Devizes, serving as the only county prison until 1631. Originally the county justices had hoped to erect it in the castle grounds, but they eventually chose the present Grange site in Bridewell Street. A new lock-up was also built at the back of the Wool Hall in 1655 and later incorporated into the back of the Town Hall. Borough records often refer to repairs to the cucking stool for scolds, which was obviously in frequent use. The gallows was situated at the end of the ditch in the present Hillworth Road and suicides were usually buried there outside the parish boundary. Sometimes 'rough justice' was used to condemn lewd behaviour. In

1560 James Tanner and his pregnant lover Kathryn Harrys were 'led about the town with basons' clashed together to draw attention to their immorality, and hounded out of town. Parish overseers spent much time chasing up the fathers of illegitimate children to force them to support their offspring rather than leave the task to the parish. Sometimes the streets resounded to the 'hue and cry', when the residents were called out to pursue and catch thieves; if they failed, the town would be fined by the sheriff.

In 1523 John Bent, an Urchfont tailor and Lollard sympathizer, was burnt to death in Devizes market place for his religious beliefs. He had asserted that the body of Christ was not present in the sacrament and that going on pilgrimages and making offerings to saints were a waste of money. To the established Church all this was dangerous heresy. The sixteenth century was a time of religious upheaval in the country, with the new Protestant doctrines challenging traditional Catholic teachings and ritual. The differing religious policies followed during the reigns of Edward VI, Mary I and Elizabeth I led to abrupt alterations in church services and furnishings. The progress of these radical changes, which took place within a generation and must have been bewildering to the ordinary parishioner, can be traced in St Mary's churchwardens' accounts. In 1550, during the Protestant phase in Edward VI's reign, the churchwardens spent 14d on 'plucking down the altars' and 4s 8d for a new Book of Common Prayer. Three years later, with Catholic Mary on the throne, they had to restore the altars, cross, images and rood loft and buy frankincense and holy oil. The Scriptures and Ten Commandments, which had been inscribed on the walls during Edward's reign, were erased. Then when Elizabeth I became Queen, Protestant liturgy and doctrines were in favour once more. The church and chancel were whitewashed, the Ten Commandments restored to the walls, the rood loft, organ and candlesticks were removed and a Book of Protestant Martyrs was chained in the church.

The growth of extreme Protestantism or Puritanism in the late sixteenth century and early seventeenth century and increased Parliamentary opposition to the use of the Royal prerogative by the Stuart kings, combined to create the circumstances leading to the English Civil War. Devizes was also to play its part in this drama.

CHAPTER 5

Men in Visors

Devizes lay in a strategic position on the road between Charles I's headquarters at Oxford and the south-west where his cause was strong. It was thus a prize worth capturing by each side in the Civil War. Despite the town's two MPs, Edward Bayntun and Robert Nicholas, being supporters of Parliament and the heavy exactions of ship money by the King in 1635 and 1638, there was strong Royalist sympathy within Devizes, led by the Mayor, Richard Pierce, a draper and owner of The Swan. Although Sir Edward Bayntun had repaired some of the castle's fortifications, said in 1596 to be 'ruinated', the town was occupied early in 1643 by Colonel Lunsford in the name of the King. The chamberlains' accounts for 1642-3 show that Devizes was busily preparing for a Parliamentary attack, items of expenditure including payments for corslets, pikes, muskets, powder and swords and 'two great guns called Draks'. The Brittox was repaired and locks, chains and barricades were placed across the road entering the town from London.

In 1643, as part of Charles I's strategy of a three-pronged attack on London from the north, midlands and west, Sir Ralph Hopton and his infantry were advancing through the west country from Cornwall. During the early summer they fought a series of engagements with Sir William Waller's forces in Somerset, culminating in the indecisive battle of Lansdown near Bath on 5 July. But the Royalists had suffered heavy losses of cavalry and ammunition, and Hopton had been crippled and partially blinded by the explosion of a powder magazine. They decided, therefore, to make for Devizes where Hopton could recover, before resuming the march to Oxford. As a contemporary poem entitled 'The Second Western Wonder' put it:

Engraving of Sir Ralph Hopton.

> As for honest Sir Ralph
> It blew him to the Vyze
> Without beard or eyes

Hopton's 2,000 strong Cornish infantry were pursued by Waller's forces, and a series of running fights took place between

Richard Pierce, Mayor of Devizes 1642-3.

Engraving of Sir William Waller, Parliamentary general.

Chippenham and Devizes, including a skirmish at the ford behind Rowdeford House. Hopton was put to bed in the dilapidated Devizes castle and the town prepared for a siege. Waller camped with some relief near Roundway village as his men had been fighting continuously for ten days, but they managed to disperse a Royalist party coming from Oxford with much-needed bullets and match; 200 prisoners and fifteen loads of ammunition were taken.

Although the Mayor, Richard Pierce, revealed to Hopton the store of powder that had been secreted in St John's church, the shortage of ammunition was now serious, and on 10 July it was decided to send a small cavalry force under the Marquis of Hertford to fetch guns, powder and bullets from Oxford. In fact four regiments were already on their way to join Hertford but, failing to meet him, turned back when only 5 miles from Devizes. Despite being attacked by Waller's horse and losing eighteen prisoners, Hertford reached Oxford on 11 July, and the Royalists set out again with about 1,800 cavalry and two small guns. Meanwhile Captain Pope 'came verie pensive' to Sir Ralph Hopton and informed him that he had only 150lbs of match left. Hopton ordered that all the bed cords in the town were to be seized and boiled in resin to make match, and he also had lead stripped from the church roofs for making bullets.

Waller now set up a battery of seven guns on Jump Hill and bombarded the town. According to Hopton, he 'day and night poured great and small shott into us'. A cannon ball was found in the belfry of St James's church in 1780 and twenty-seven of his canister shot grazed the tower of St. John's church and the wall of the Beauchamp chapel, fourteen of them in a space two feet square. Waller's attack on the town on 12 July was delayed by heavy

Waller bombards Devizes from Jump Hill: a drawing by James Waylen.

morning rain, but in the afternoon, after four hours of fierce fighting, the Parliamentary horse charged into the outer streets, getting as far as Morris Lane, where they were held up by heavy timber barricades. Waller now demanded the surrender of the castle, but Hopton, expecting the arrival of reinforcements, played for time, and so Waller drew off his forces to take up position astride the downs road from Oxford along which his scouts had informed him the Royalists were coming. At 4 p.m. on Thursday 13 July, the Cavalier forces reached Roundway Down, having fired a gun when passing over Roughridge Hill to alert Hopton to their arrival. But Hopton's officers, fearing a trick, advised him to remain in the castle, and so the Royalists faced a force roughly three times their own strength, consisting of 3,000 foot in the centre, with 2,000 horse, 500 dragoons and 8 field guns on the wings. Waller was supremely confident, in fact sending a message to Parliament that 'by the next post he would send the number and quality of his prisoners'.

The battle took place on the open down between Roundway Hill, Morgan's Hill, King's Play Hill and Roughridge Hill. The initial attack on the Royalists by Sir Arthur Hazelrigg and his famous 'Lobsters', so called because they were completely covered in armour, was repulsed and their cannon were captured. Sir John Byron's brigade then advanced, bravely holding their fire until the Roundheads had spent all their shot, and then 'gave them ours in their teeth'. Despite attacking up a slope, the Cavaliers put the Parliamentary cavalry to flight within half an hour, pursuing them with exhilaration for 3 miles across the open down towards the semi-precipitous drop of about 300 ft into what has become known locally as the 'Bloody Ditch'. Hopton's forces, emerging from Devizes to join the fray, could see 'the enemy's whole body of horse face about and runne with speede and our horse in close bodye fyring in their reare till they had chased them down the hill in a steep place where never horse went down or up before'. Sir John Byron reported that 'many of them broke their own and their horses' necks'. Waller himself is supposed to have rolled down the hill but was unhurt. The Parliamentary infantry, hitherto helpless spectators of the cavalry engagement, were now attacked by Hopton's Cornish infantry and 'thought it not fit to stay any longer'. Some six hundred were killed, the rest being wounded or captured with their arms, colours and nine brass cannon. The Calne parish register records on July 1643 the burial of 'three soldiers which were wounded to death upon the Vize Down in the fight there' and William Bartlett, of Chirton, a quartermaster in

Shot holes in the walls of St John's church made during Waller's bombardment of the town.

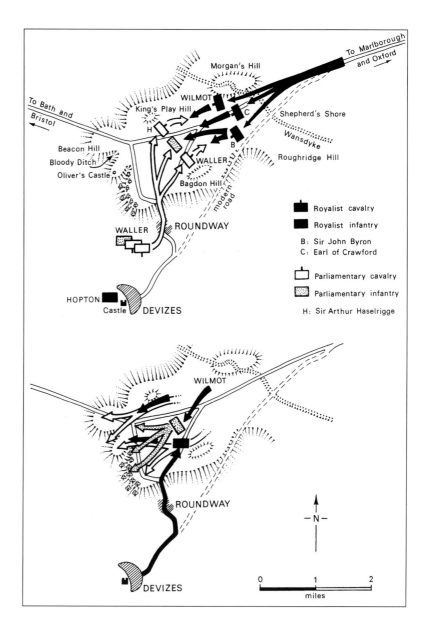

The map legend contains:

- Royalist cavalry
- Royalist infantry
- B: Sir John Byron
- C: Earl of Crawford
- Parliamentary cavalry
- Parliamentary infantry
- H: Sir Arthur Haselrigge

Plans of the Battle of Roundway Down, 13 July 1643. (Nick Griffiths)

Colonel Sandys' regiment, was buried at Rowde on 14 July. Some shallow grave pits have been found on Roundway Down containing skeletons with bullet and sabre wounds. But where the bodies of the rest of the slain were buried remains a mystery.

Waller fled to Bristol, taking the news of his 'mischance', though he admitted that 'it was the most heavy stroke that ever did befall me'. All his baggage, artillery and ammunition had been captured, together with a cart laden with manacles, curiously described in a Parliamentary broadsheet as 'for the liberty of the subject'. For the Royalists, the Battle of Roundway Down marked the high point of their fortunes. Parliament's western army had been almost annihilated and the victory led to the fall of Malmesbury and Bristol to the King; had it also been followed by the capture of Gloucester it could have proved the turning point of the war. The Cavaliers renamed it 'the Battle of Runaway' and took to wearing a piece of cord in their hatbands to remind them of the boiling of the bedcords, which had provided match at a critical time. The battle took its place in local folklore; the Rowde parish register noted on 13 July 'a cloud like a lion rampant azure was on the army fighting'.

Devizes remained under Royalist control until 1645. Hoping to recoup his fortunes in the west country, Charles I sent Sir Charles Lloyd, his chief engineer and quartermaster general, to refortify Devizes castle. The constables of Potterne and Cannings Hundreds were summoned to assemble 200 able-bodied men with spades, mattocks, shovels, and carts and horses for one month's work at the castle; they had to be provided with food and accommodation in houses and barns in the town. Stockades and palisades were erected, the moat was cleared out and the drawbridge repaired. Some four hundred Welshmen now garrisoned the castle ready to face Oliver Cromwell who was campaigning in the area with 5,000 troops. Having lured Sir James Long and the Royalist cavalry, who might relieve the siege, into a trap, Cromwell demanded the surrender of the castle. The garrison sent out a dog previously belonging to Prince Rupert, with a poem attached to its neck, the gist of which was:

> The Welshmen they do swear apace
> They'll die before they yield this place

Cromwell's response was to bombard the castle day and night with ten guns stationed in the market-place. On 23 September, when a shell landed in the roofless keep where the powder was stored, Sir Charles Lloyd surrendered, and he and his officers were allowed to join the King at Oxford. The castle had evidently been provisioned for a long siege. It was found to contain 400 stand of arms, and provisions sufficient for a year, including 500 barrels of beef, 500 flitches of bacon and 120 fat sheep.

The castle's capture, which had cost the besieging army just five men, was regarded by the Roundheads as sweet revenge for their defeat at Roundway Down and an important strategic coup. A public thanksgiving service was held in London on the following Sunday, and Cromwell ordered the Army Committee to pay £10 to the messenger who brought 'the good news of taking of the

The Castle of The Devises from y^e north West.

John Strachey's sketch of Devizes castle mound, 1730.

Devizes'. In 1646 Parliament ordered that the castle should be 'slighted', although this was not actually carried out until 1648. When John Strachey made a survey of Devizes castle grounds in 1730 he drew a large mound and an orchard, with the pit of the powder house and a dilapidated stone house in the grounds. The drawbridge had gone and the ditch was filled up. In the eighteenth century it became a source of building material for local people; William Stukeley wrote in 1724: 'the castle is ignobly mangled and every day destroyed by persons who care not to leave a stone standing, though for a wall to their gardens'.

The lives of some who had fought in the war were also shattered. Rowland Humfrey, a yeoman of St Mary's parish, was a corporal in Sir Charles Lloyd's regiment. He claimed a pension from Charles II for the wounds he had received in the Royal cause. He had been:

... 'shot in the head in the fight at Newbury, and shot in the hand, shot through the leg at Killington Green, wounded in the knee at Banbury, wounded in the left arm in Cornwall, received one great Cutt with a sword in the handwrist att the taking of Bristol for King Charles, and alsoe a great blow with a muskett in the mouth which beate out allmost all his teeth, beside the cutting of his hippes at the siege of Reading; all of which said woundes and blows hath soe decayed your petitioner's body that he is thereby made almost unfitt for any bodily labour to support his wife and two children.'

It is clear too that the life of Devizes had been much disrupted by the war. Soldiers were billeted in the churches and the Shambles, and both sides commandeered money, supplies and horses, and conscripted men. In 1647 Devizes weavers complained that their apprentices were running away to join 'some army or garrison'. The year before, the tithings of Roundway, Wick, Nursteed and Bedborough protested that 'they were so disabled by being so much plundered ... that they are not able to relieve their own poore'. To compound the problem the town had been visited by plague in 1644. Stallholders in the market had their goods seized and Sir Charles Lloyd set on fire the houses of four people who refused to co-operate. Townspeople were forced to act as scouts and fetch ammunition from other towns, while clothiers taking their goods to London for sale were made by the Cavaliers to pay an excise of £400 for their safe passage. In 1828, when an old house was being pulled down, a hundred silver coins dating from the reigns of Mary, Elizabeth, James I and Charles I were discovered in a pot under a hearth stone, possibly hidden by some canny townsman determined not to be impoverished by the greedy demands of the rival armies. Soldiers quartered in the town in 1646 caused an uproar in St John's church: 'divers soldiers armed in a most irreverent manner to the abominable disturbance of the whole congregation' ordered the Presbyterian rector out of the pulpit, saying that he was 'unfit to preach'. It was these soldiers, with their radical political and religious opinions, who encouraged the establishment of Anabaptist meetings in the town. In 1654 local Baptists who were attempting to hold a baptism ceremony in the Crammer were set upon by a local mob, who tried to throw them all in the pond.

The establishment of the Puritan Commonwealth brought many changes. Marriages now took place in front of a JP instead of in church. Christmas celebrations were banned, and in 1655 a Devizes man was sent to the House of Correction 'for singing of ballets [ballads] contrary to the Statute'. Joan Read, wife of a weaver, complained at the Quarter Sessions that two persons had reported her as being a witch, and in consequence two bakers in the town had forbidden her to come into their bake-house for dough. Prejudice and bitterness were rife. Just as the Cavaliers had destroyed Bromham House and Southbroom House, residences of Roundhead supporters, so after the war Parliament punished Richard Pierce, the Mayor, and Michael Tidcombe, an attorney, for collecting money for the King. The return of the monarchy in 1660 was greeted in Devizes with some relief. The church bells were rung, guns were fired and the Corporation spent £5 on a venison feast to celebrate 'His Majesty's Happy Restauracon'.

Controversy, however, continued to divide Devizes in the later Stuart period, as it did the country. The political and religious divisions of the Civil War developed on party lines, with the formation of the Court or Tory party, largely Anglican and opposed to further restriction of the King's power, and the Country or Whig party, many of whom were Nonconformists, who wished to curb the Royal prerogative further. The increasing control of Parliament over the purse strings made it important for the King to secure the return of MPs favourable to his cause, and both Charles II and James II tampered with the borough charters, including those of Devizes, to achieve a pliant House of Commons. Devizes was a Corporation borough - that is, the right to vote in parliamentary elections was restricted to the Council. It therefore became a matter of some importance to each faction to gain control of the Corporation and so influence the election result. After 1694 parliamentary elections were held every three years, so party feeling had little chance to die down. As the mayor presided over the election his office gained a new political significance. MPs also had access to the strings of patronage and could do much to further their supporters' economic and political interests. Local government therefore became infected with party feeling.

Although the names Whig and Tory were not used in borough politics, there was much factional in-fighting. One cause of dispute was who elected the MPs, all the burgesses or just the senior burgesses. Between 1660 and 1707 eight parliamentary elections were challenged and referred to the House of Commons Committee of Privileges. Election of local officers also aroused fierce rivalry. At the election of a coroner in the Wool Hall in 1698 the supporters of one candidate tried to deter his rival's voters by forcing them to leave the Hall by the window down an old ladder. More farcical scenes occurred in 1707. On 29 September John Eyles, the Whig mayor-elect, went to be sworn in at the Guildhall, accompanied by the outgoing mayor and twenty-one councillors. But a rival faction, including the recorder and ten other councillors, swore in another mayor, Richard Bundy Franklin, at the Wool Hall. The following Thursday excitement had reached such a pitch that some farmers, disgruntled at having to pay market tolls, attacked the outgoing mayor and his followers, shouting such 'low expressions' as 'Why don't we kick the guts of them out', and drove them from the market place. On the next Sunday, when the new mayor, John Eyles, arrived at St Mary's church for the mayoral service, he discovered that the rival mayor had been sitting in the mayor's pew for two hours. Franklin, being forcibly ejected from the seat, then stood in front of the mayor for the whole service, blocking his view. In the afternoon, a similar scene was enacted in

St John's church amid much mutual verbal abuse. Trying to assert his right to the mayor's pew, Franklin put his head between the aged mayor's legs, lifted him up and would have thrown him on to the floor had he not been restrained. Franklin afterwards claimed that he had been knocked about in the melée and pretended that he was lame, but rather spoilt the effect by drinking punch that night with a friend who lived some distance away. The rector reported the disturbance to the Bishop of Salisbury, who referred the matter to the Secretary of State, the Earl of Sunderland, describing it as 'a great tumult'. Legal proceedings dragged on for several months but eventually, after a petition to Queen Anne from leading townsmen, a new mayor was elected. The final melodramatic touch to the whole affair occurred in 1709 when Henry Bishop, imprisoned for his part in 'the notorious riot in the market place', was rescued by two men in visors.

CHAPTER 6

Georgian Devizes: The Golden Age

St John's Street in the early eighteenth century from a painting showing the Wool Hall (centre) on the site of the present Town Hall.

The long dominance of the Whig party during the early Georgian period did much to dampen party feeling and the eighteenth century was a time of great economic prosperity for Devizes. It was perhaps the last period in which Devizes could claim to be a cloth town. Owing to German and Dutch competition, the old white cloth trade had declined, and clothiers had turned to the production of 'the new draperies' such as medleys and drugget, lightly woven cloths introduced from France in the late seventeenth century. In 1726, Daniel Defoe reported that Devizes had 'run pretty much into the drugget making trade', and it is significant that when he needed an example of the drugget trade for his book *The Complete English Tradesman* he chose Devizes. During the period 1700 - 1730, seven drugget makers were admitted as freemen of the Drapers' Guild, along with twelve woolstaplers and sixteen clothiers. When Defoe mentioned that Devizes was 'full of wealthy clothiers' he was referring to the great clothier dynasties of the town, such as the Webbs, Paradices and Suttons, and Stephen Hillman, the Devizes wool merchant, who was worth £800 a year.

John Anstie's cloth factory in New Park Street photographed in the 1980s when it was used by Woodwards the printers.

Edward Dore's map of Devizes of 1759 illustrates the preoccupation of the town with the wool trade, showing drying racks for cloth in the fields on the outskirts of the town.

In the mid-eighteenth century, the serge trade declined; after 1725 no serge makers were admitted to the Drapers' Guild. It was replaced by the production of an extra fine luxury cloth called 'cassimere', blended from silk, wool, cotton and mohair, which had been invented by a Bradford-on-Avon clothier. Pre-eminent among the specialists in this trade was John Anstie. Receptive to the new technological developments, he built one of the first factories in the west of England in New Park Street, where he installed twenty spinning jennies and three hundred weaving looms, employing large numbers of men, women and children to make cloth for the fashionable London market as well as for European crowned heads. But the export trade was adversely affected by the French war and John Anstie's bankruptcy in 1793 was a great economic blow to the town. Although Robert Waylen and Peter Walker carried on silk and cloth production until 1828, Devizes never recovered its position as a cloth town. The increasing use of water power to run the heavier machines meant that Devizes was at a disadvantage compared with towns like Trowbridge and Bradford-on-Avon, which were situated by fast flowing streams.

Other trades, however, continued to grow and flourish. Between 1660 and 1819, there were thirty clockmakers in Devizes, more than in any other Wiltshire town. James Burrough, whose bell foundry was on the site of The Ark in Long Street, made bells for many Wiltshire churches, as well as casting two of the bells of nearby St John's church. There were still leather traders in the town, such as Joseph Baster, a glover and breeches maker, who lived next to The Queen's Head on Dunkirk Hill, and had his shop in Northgate Street and lime and tan pits at the entrance to Conscience Lane. He 'wore in' a new pair of breeches every Sunday when he went to the Congregational church because, as he said, they 'sold better'. Other traders were becoming established such as booksellers, milliners, grocers, chemists, cabinet makers and silversmiths, illustrating the growing significance of commerce to the economy and the increasing wealth and sophistication of the burgesses. Many traders diversified. Isaac Newton, a staymaker, also sold books, stationery, medicines and perfumery and ran a circulating library. Although the Mercers Guild had been dissolved in 1769, tradesmen were still prepared to defend their interests. In 1773, armed with cleavers, marrow bones, and horns, they saw off a travelling linen draper who had distributed handbills in the town.

During the eighteenth century, the foundations were laid for Devizes becoming a 'beer and baccy' town. Brewing and malting had been carried on for centuries, and some inns continued to brew their own beer into the twentieth century. The firm of Figgins and Gent was established in Bridewell Street in the mid-eighteenth century, later to become Rose and Tylee, and then Tylee and Gent; by 1783, half the forty one Devizes pubs were their tied houses. In the early nineteenth century, the firm moved to the Maltings in Northgate Street, and eventually merged in the Wadworth Brewery. Edward Dore's map of 1759 noted that 'the tobacco trade has increased of late'. This was due to the enterprise of John Anstie, father of the clothier, who co-operated with William Leach in using two windmills on the site of Devizes castle for snuff grinding; under the shrewd direction of his son, Benjamin Webb Anstie, the business greatly expanded in the latter part of the Georgian period.

But it was the market above all which shaped the future of Devizes. *The Salisbury Journal* in February 1793 described Devizes as

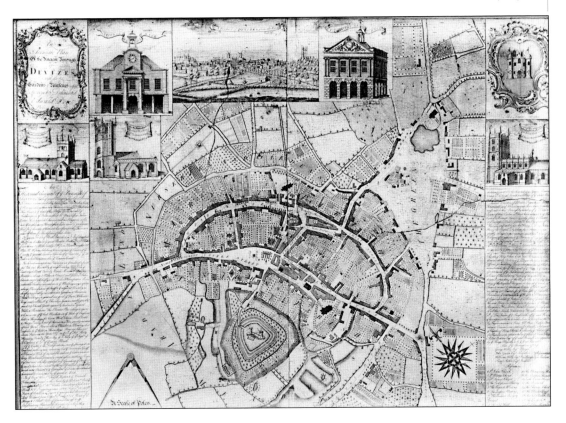

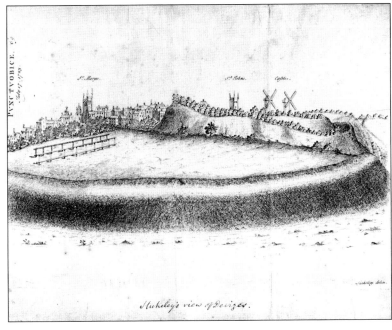

Edward Dore's map of Devizes , 1759. Scale: 40" to 1 mile.

William Stukeley's drawing of windmills on the castle mound, 1723.

'one of the best market towns in the west of England'. The Monday market specialised in butchers' meat; on Thursdays, meat, corn, wool, horses and cattle were sold, and from 1776 a monthly cattle market was established. During the eighteenth century, Devizes became one of the premier corn markets of the kingdom, its prices being regularly quoted in the London newspapers. The corn market was held between 12 noon and 1.30 p.m., half an hour earlier in winter, and its beginning was announced by the ringing of a bell. On Thursday 25 January 1753, the market place was the scene of a famous incident. Ruth Pierce of Potterne agreed with three other women to buy a sack of wheat, sharing the cost between them, but the woman collecting the money soon discovered that she was 3d short and demanded the residue from Ruth Pierce. She protested that she had paid her share, and wished she might drop down dead if she had not, whereupon she did. The inquest concluded that she had been struck down dead by the vengeance of God with a lie in her mouth. A painted board recording the incident was fixed to the market house and later a similar inscription was incorporated in the present market cross, with the additional (fabricated) phrase 'having the money concealed in her hand' to point the moral further.

Two developments underline the expansion and prosperity of Devizes business in the late eighteenth century. In 1775, the first Devizes bank was opened by James Sutton, William Leach, John Bevan and Richard Read and a growing number of professional men such as attorneys, physicians and surgeons became established in the town. Traders were also migrating to Devizes from Salisbury and London to set up business. Many of these affluent citizens were influential in improving the visual aspect of Devizes by architectural and civic renovation. Although its powers were limited, the Improvement Commission set up in 1780 made a start on erecting lamps and watch boxes and cleaning the streets. Some cobbled roads were 'pitched' or paved, and it seems that some of the stones from Avebury, which was then being dismantled, were used for this purpose. The Chamberlains' accounts for 1805 and 1806 record payments to 'Mr Erwood for bringing sarsen stones and flints from Avebury'. At the cost of some archaeological vandalism, therefore, Devizes was striving to acquire a more modern appearance in keeping with its growing prosperity.

Devizes is a good example of a Georgian brick-built town. Within the space of a quarter of a mile, there are nearly five hundred listed buildings, many of them constructed or re-fronted in the eighteenth century because of the generation of local wealth among business and professional men. Brick earth was obtainable locally, but until

Brownston House, built earlier than the 1720 date on the rainwater head. An early-eighteenth-century rent book refers to Francis Merewether's 'new built house, now Thomas Browne's.'

the opening of the Kennet and Avon canal in 1810, Bath stone was difficult and therefore expensive to transport; it was used sparingly only for frontages and window dressings and for prestige buildings. Brownston House, one of the two Grade I listed houses in Devizes, was built for Francis Merewether on the site of an older house; in 1720 it was occupied by Thomas Browne, a barrister and later by the Garth family, two members of whom were the town's MPs. It has particularly fine red rubbed brickwork with limestone dressings and is described by Nicholas Pevsner as 'the best house in Devizes'. The other Grade I house, 17, Market Place, was built in Queens Anne's

No. 17 Market Place, contemporary with Brownston House.

Parnella House with a statue of Aesculapius over the door.

reign for an attorney, Wadham Locke. It has fine plaster ceilings, wood carved friezes and good ironwork in front of the house. On the opposite side of the road Parnella House, faced with stone, was the home of the Clare family of surgeons, who advertised their profession with a statue of Aesculapius, the Greek god of healing, over the door. Most of the other buildings in the market place betray their eighteenth-century origins from the first floor upwards.

Long Street has perhaps the most homogeneous and consistently high quality architecture in the town. In the eighteenth century it became the most fashionable residential area. The houses on the west side, including the Rectory, are Georgian, usually double fronted, often with Doric porticoes and large gardens, but of the houses on the east side, number 8, dating from 1737, is one of the few with a sizeable garden. This was the house of Joseph Needham,

Georgian houses in Long Street. Lansdowne House is the white, stuccoed house on the right.

described in *The Salisbury Journal* as 'the most celebrated man-midwife in the kingdom'. It is a brick house with stone front, and originally also had a statue of Aesculapius over the door. No. 30 Long Street, now the Conservative Club, was bought for a member of the Sutton family, Robert, whose son was one of the managers of the original London Stock Exchange. It seems unlikely that Lansdowne House had any direct connection with the Lansdowne family; Lord Lansdowne would hardly need a Devizes town house when he lived so near at Bowood. The late eighteenth-century brick house was occupied by Samuel Adlam, a clothier; his daughter married Revd Henry Bayntun, who constructed the present white stuccoed façade in 1809. His position as non-resident Vicar of Bromham for sixty-three years perhaps explains the compliment to Lord Lansdowne. Many of the other houses on the east side of Long Street retain their old timber structure, but were refaced with plaster fronts and given new sash windows; as the local saying goes, they were 'Queen Anne in front and Mary Anne behind'. Some indeed have internal stonework with chevron moulding, perhaps inserted when the castle was being demolished in the seventeenth century.

In 1731, Greystone House in High Street was built in brick with a Bath stone front by James Sutton I, the clothier, for the marriage of his son, Prince. Barford House in St John's Street has interesting local brickwork in red and blue; in this area too the houses have long gardens running down to the castle ditch. Colour washed or stuccoed eighteenth-century inns include The Black Swan, the Lamb and the Bear, with its eighteenth-century front to a

Timber framing revealed during refurbishment of a house in Long Street.

sixteenth-century building. New Park Street seems to have been the residential area for traders and manufacturers, for example No. 39 was John Anstie's house. Northgate House, originally an inn called The King's Arms, and later the Assize Judge's lodgings, Sandcliffe, in Bath stone, and The Red House, formerly called Belle Vue, are other eighteenth-century houses further from the centre of the town.

The two major Georgian houses in the district were Southbroom House on the Green, rebuilt in Bath stone in 1773 on a new site further from the road by retired East India Company governor Edward Eyles, and New Park, later Roundway House. In 1775 James Sutton II, head of the clothier family, inherited the Roundway estate and began building New Park, designed by James Wyatt and with the grounds landscaped by Humphrey Repton, who has left this description of the estate.

... 'All the materials of natural landscape seem to be collected if not actually displayed within the pale of this beautiful park. It presents every possible variety of shape in the ground, from the cheerful and extended plan to the steep hill and abrupt precipice. The surface is everywhere enriched with wood of various growth and species, either collected in ample masses or lightly scattered in groups and single trees. Such are the natural advantages of the ground, to which must be added the richest prospects of distant country; and when nature has been thus bountiful, art has lent assistance under the direction of Mr James Wyatt, to decorate the scene with a building of the most elegant form. The house at New Park is a lasting monument to the contrivance and good taste of that ingenious architect'.

It was through James Sutton that Devizes became closely associated with a future Prime Minister. He married Eleanor, sister of Henry Addington, and James Sutton used his local influence to get Addington elected as Recorder and MP for the town, which he continued to represent until his elevation to the peerage as Viscount Sidmouth in 1805. Addington became the youngest Speaker of the House of Commons in 1789 at the age of thirty-two, and was a close friend of William Pitt the Younger, who was a frequent visitor to New Park. Although a man of sincerity and integrity, Addington was a reactionary Tory, who hated Liberalism and opposed parliamentary reform and the abolition of the slave trade. As Home Secretary, he implemented the repressive policy of the Six Acts and employed Oliver the Spy as an *agent provocateur*. He was Prime Minister from 1801 to 1804, although one MP remarked that he was as fitted for the post as one of the doorkeepers. He was, however, popular in Devizes, and in 1791 gave £500 to rebuild the Shambles, and

Henry Addington,
1st Viscount Sidmouth.

New Park, later
Roundway House.

Drawing of the Market Cross erected in the Market Place in 1814.

somewhat more reluctantly donated the present market cross in 1814, to which the Ruth Pierce tablet was later affixed. In 1826, Leg o'Mutton Street was renamed Sidmouth Street in his honour. During the period 1747 to 1832, one of the two Devizes parliamentary seats was always held by a member of the New Park family or its associates; the other was usually filled by a local merchant or someone with local connections, contrary to the general trend of control by a wealthy peer.

Civic pride found its expression in the construction of two new town halls in the Georgian period. In 1752, the 'New Hall' was built on piazzas on the site of the old Guildhall in Wine Street. It functioned as a market house, the cheese market being transferred there, and during the rebuilding of the Wool Hall, it was used for council and court business. The Wool Hall in St John's Street had a council chamber added to it in the years 1733 to 1735, and in 1792 the open courtyard was enclosed. But in 1803, the architect, James Wyatt, reported that the fabric of the Wool Hall was in a 'very dangerous and alarming situation', and was not worth repairing. A new town hall was therefore built on the same site between 1806 and 1808. The architect was Thomas Baldwin, designer of Bath Guildhall, but local tradesmen were used for masonry, tiling and plasterwork, the main contractor being Benoni White, the town's leading builder at that time. George Dyke, landlord of the nearby Scribbling Horse, now The Lamb, was imprisoned for six months in the Bridewell for helping himself to tiles, stone and planks from the demolished building, which he possibly used for re-fronting his inn. The town hall was built of

The New Hall (centre), erected in 1752 on the site of the old Guildhall.

Bath stone, with a rusticated ground floor and an iron balcony and included a cheese hall and council chamber, as well as a splendid assembly room in the style of Adam, with a musicians' gallery. The rear of the old building was retained to provide a jury room. At the foundation stone ceremony in 1806, a brass plate and an eight-inch square lead box containing a parchment listing the names of the Corporation were placed in the circular projection facing the market place. This box was found during repairs in 1922 and another brass plate was added to it. The total cost of the building was £6,416, of which the two borough MPs, Joshua Smith and Thomas Estcourt, each contributed £1,000. The portraits of George III and Queen Charlotte in the assembly room were presented twenty years later by George Watson Taylor. On November 2nd 1808, the Town Hall was opened with a grand ball and supper for three hundred guests. A year later, the marble bust of Addington was placed in the council chamber.

The Town Hall became the venue for fashionable monthly winter assemblies. Although Edward Gibbon, sent to Devizes in 1761 as a captain in the South Hampshire militia, described the town as inhospitable, there seems to have been ample entertainment. There was frequent civic feasting, to celebrate elections, coronations, wars and peace. At the mayor's feast in 1774, the guests consumed 77lbs of beef, 2 quarters of lamb, 1 sturgeon, 5 turbots, 4 cods, 4 sucking pigs, 4 turkeys, 12 ducks, 36 fowls, 4 geese, 20 tongues and 7 pigeon pies, followed by rich cakes, fruit, puddings and mince pies. At the new theatre built on the Green in 1792 to replace the old cramped quarters in Monday Market Street, Shatford and Lee's Salisbury company performed such delights as 'The Grand Spectacle of George IV's Coronation' and 'The Vampire' set on the island of Staffa, with special scenic effects and 'a descension of the Spirit of the Air'. For the less artistically inclined, there was bull baiting at Furzehill, where in 1774 Ezekiel Robbins aged 14 killed himself by drinking rum, as well as single stick playing, and backsword contests for a prize of five guineas on a stage opposite The Bear. The Bear Club, founded in 1756, combined convivial weekly meetings at that hostelry with the provision of education and apprenticeships for poor town boys and this institution typifies the underlying philanthropic spirit of the eighteenth century. The accounts of the Overseers of the Poor of St Mary's parish record, not only payments to the local indigent poor, such as 'clothing Clack's children when they had the Itch '(smallpox), but also discretionary grants such as 'two shillings to a stranger, a native of Russia', 'two shillings and sixpence to an

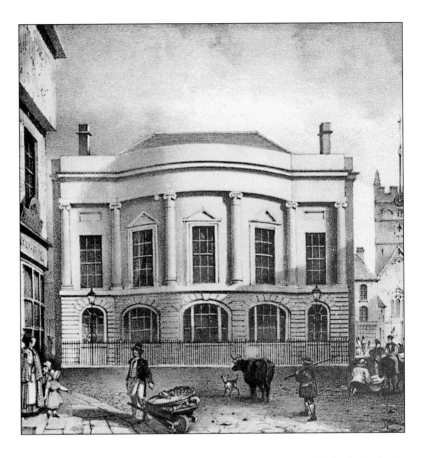

The Town Hall in the mid-nineteenth century.

American family in distress' and 'two guineas to a Turkish Pasha'.

The eighteenth century witnessed the expansion of Nonconformity in Devizes. The presence of Roundhead soldiers in the town during the Commonwealth period had led to the establishment of groups of Baptists, who worshipped in a tenement building behind No. 22, The Brittox. After the Restoration, however, the Cavalier Parliament persecuted the Nonconformists, and a number of Presbyterian ministers ejected from their livings took refuge in Devizes, where Dissent spread rapidly among the cloth workers. In 1670, the Bishop of Salisbury urged the JPs to suppress the 'great and outrageous meetings in the town', although the magistrates denied that any such meetings were causing trouble. Quakerism too gained a foothold in Devizes and the burial ground in Hillworth Park dates from the late seventeenth century. In 1678 Bishops Cannings register recorded that Quakers were buried 'near Gallows Ditch' and it is known that three Quakers from Devizes accompanied William Penn to Pennsylvania in 1683.

The Nonconformists were excluded from borough government, but after the Toleration Act of 1689, which required the licensing of their meeting houses, they seem to have been allowed freedom of worship. The arrival of a High Church Rector, Revd William Wells and his equally intolerant curate, Revd Edward Innes, however, changed the ambivalent attitude. When John Wesley visited the town in October 1747, the curate had been indefatigably stirring up the mob to disrupt his meetings, setting up an advertisement of 'an obnubilative pantomime and entertainment to be exhibited at Mr Clark's' where Wesley was to preach. John Wesley described the town as being 'in an uproar from end to end as if the French were just entering and an abundance of swelling words were heard, with oaths, curses and threatenings'. Worse was to come on his brother Charles's visit in February 1748. The church bells were rung backwards and the curate's mob laid siege for three hours to the house where Charles was preaching and praying, tearing down shutters and roof tiles, and playing a fire hose into one of the rooms. Plied with ale by local Tory gentlemen, the mob set free the visitors' horses, which were found some hours later standing terrified up to their chins in the pond. Eventually Charles Wesley and his friends escaped up the Bath Road, escorted by a constable and pursued by the mob with two bulldogs. Charles commented sadly in his journal, 'Such diabolical malice I have not seen in human faces'. A generation later, however, John Wesley was able to preach 'very quietly at the Devizes' and declared that 'the furious prejudice which long reigned in this town is now vanished away'.

During the later Georgian period, Nonconformity continued to spread, and various denominations established chapels in the town. The open air preaching of Rowland Hill led to the foundation of a Congregational chapel in Northgate Street in 1776, and the Baptists, outgrowing their meeting house in the Brittox, built a new chapel in Maryport Street four years later. The Presbyterians and a group of seceding Baptists combined in 1792 to erect a meeting house in Sheep Street near the present Baptist church, and this group was to become the nucleus of the New Baptist congregation in the next century. Many of the leading businessmen of the town were Nonconformists, who took an active part in the growing agitation for political reform and wider participation in government, as well as contributing much to the economic progress of Devizes.

The original Baptist meeting house behind 22 The Brittox, before recent rebuilding.

CHAPTER 7

Inns & Travel

The importance of Devizes as a market town enhanced the status of inns, which became centres of social and commercial life. From Tudor times, JPs had frequently recommended the suppression of alehouses because of a shortage of grain, but in 1766 as many as forty-one inns and alehouses were recorded in Devizes, twenty-six in the New Port, eleven in the Old Port and four on the Green. Eight inns are traceable back to the sixteenth century or earlier; The Bear, The Lamb, The Hart, The Crown, The Salutation, The Swan, The Angel and The Lion. Of these, possibly the oldest is The Hart in St John's Alley, mentioned in the reign of Richard II. Former pub sites are commemorated in street names such as The Chequer, Cross Keys Yard and Old Swan Yard. The name of The Bear probably stems from association with the Earl of Warwick, a thirteenth-century governor of the castle, whose emblem was a bear and ragged staff. Some inn names emphasize the importance of the cloth trade to the town, such as The Fleece, The Hand and Shears, The Scribbling Horse and The Woolpack. Many inns have changed their names over the centuries, landlords sometimes taking the name with them when they moved to another hostelry.

The most important inns were The Bear, The Crown and the Salutation, later The Elm Tree. The White Bear, which was the property of St Mary's church and was originally called The Talbot, enjoyed a good position in the old market place, with the market cross and a teasel post in front; it had an adjoining malthouse and was much used by cattle drovers. Others, like the Waggon and Horses on the site of the present garage by the canal in The Nursery and The Axe and Compass on the site of the Catholic church, were carters' stopping places on the old road to Bath. The Crown often supplied refreshments to the Corporation in the seventeenth century and a billiards room there is referred to in a will of 1694. The Three Tuns near Morris Lane in Long Street had a real tennis court and The Bear had a bowling alley and ornamental grounds. Until 1768, The Castle Inn was a private house, though there may have been an earlier inn on the site. Most of the inns had extensive stables, often on the opposite side of the road. John Aubrey in the late seventeenth century, mentioned that 'metheglyn is a pretty considerable manufacture in this town, time out of mind'. This drink, a kind of mead made from fermented honey, was produced by the Pierce family, prominent Royalists in the civil war, who kept The Swan in the High Street. The Black Swan, then next to the Shambles, was run in the early seventeenth century by James Edney. When he died in 1638, he left twenty hogsheads of metheglyn, fifteen hundredweight of honey and £6 worth of wax 'in the Meth House'. James Edney's house contained 'two joyned bedsteads, three truck bedsteads, six feather bedds, seven flock bedds, four feather bedsteads, one truck bedstead and one linen bedstead', providing extensive accommodation for travellers. A national survey of 1686, which aimed to discover how much inn accommodation could be supplied for soldiers' billets in time of war, showed that Devizes could provide ninety-seven beds and ranked sixth in the county. It could provide stabling for 525 horses, second in the county only to Salisbury.

The improvement of the roads in the eighteenth century increased the inn trade. Carriers from Devizes were already making the long journey to London in 1637, according to 'The Carrier's Cosmographie', arriving on Thursdays and returning on Fridays.

The Devizes area from Andrews' and Dury's map of Wiltshire, 1773. The old Bath Road ran along the course of the present canal, with the Besborough Lodge turnpike at the junction with Northgate Street. The Lavington, Rowde and Nursteed roads were turnpiked by this time, as was part of the London Road. The Rowde and Nursteed turnpikes are marked; other gates were at Devizes Wick and The Green.

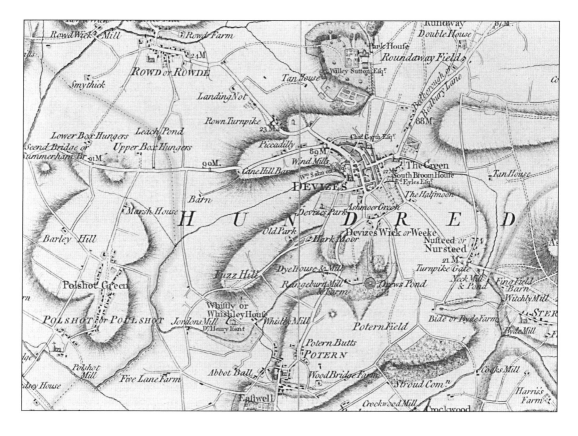

But the Turnpike Trusts opened the way for wider passenger travel and goods transport and greatly increased the importance of those inns on the cross country routes which had facilities for stabling and changing horses. John Macadam and his son are supposed to have worked on the later Devizes Turnpike Trust roads. The road from Etchilhampton via Devizes to Rowdeford was turnpiked by Act of Parliament in 1706-7 'by reason of the great and many loads and heavy carriages of Goods which are weekly drawn through the same … and being in several places thereof very Ruinous and Impassable, insomuch that it is become very Dangerous to all Persons, Horses, Cattle that pass that way'. It did not, however, cover the road within the town, and it was reported in 1724 that 'part of the road within the Borough was so bad that many of the carriages were broken on entering the town'. The Lavington to Seend road was improved 1750-1, and with the creation of a new southern exit from the town, the old Hartmoor route, with its Angel Inn, fell out of use. The new London road, superseding the old downs road, was turnpiked in 1706-7, and in 1784, with the second stretch from Wansdyke to Devizes opened in 1820. The London route passed through the town via Monday Market Street and New Park Street. Although not one of the primary roads to Bath, the Devizes route became preferable in the late eighteenth century to the Chippenham route which was infested with highwaymen. Until the making of the canal the Bath road ran along the line of the canal, rejoining the present road by the Prison Bridge. The improvement of the Andover road in 1756 was due to the enterprise of James Long, who had a new road made between Nursteed and Lydeway, avoiding the difficult former route over Etchilhampton Hill. A subscription in his honour paid for the construction of the lion monument along the new road.

Road improvements were financed by variable tolls payable at the five turnpike gates at the entrances to the town. These were the Green gate by St James's church, Nursteed gate by the Green, Potterne gate at the entrance to Wick Lane, the Seend gate at Besborough Lodge and Rowde gate near the Oxhouse. When the Big Lane and Conscience Lane routes into Devizes were abandoned in favour of Rowde Hill, as Dunkirk Hill was then called, the toll house was moved, first to the bottom and then to the top of the hill near Shane's castle, which is, however, a later building, dating from 1840. Further steps had to be taken to stop evasion of toll payment; the Nursteed gate was moved to near The Fox and Hounds, as the old Salisbury road through Brickley Lane was being used as an escape route, and bye gates were erected in Quaker's Walk, Dyehouse Lane and other side lanes.

Tolls were financially unpopular, and also caused delays, especially when sheep had to be counted, but undoubtedly the turnpiked roads were a great improvement on the previous rutted tracks, in which travellers had sometimes been known to drown. It was now possible to transport heavier loads by waggon and to link up towns by stage and mail coach routes. Flying machines, coaches which went from London to Bristol in a couple of days, halted at The Bear, which was famous, not only for its hospitality, but also for its extensive stables, which then stretched to behind The Pelican (then The New Inn). It became a fashionable stopping place on the journey to Bath, then the resort of the wits and *beau monde* of the kingdom. To cope with the increased custom, the main part of the building was re-fronted in brick, and sash windows were added, together with a columned porch and a curved Venetian staircase. A Bath stone-fronted extension was built to the south with two-storeyed bay windows and elaborate garlanded decorations. George Whatley, the landlord who died in 1767, was described in *The Salisbury Journal* as 'the most eminent publican in the west of England'.

It was Thomas Lawrence, however, who most captured the imagination in his seven year stay as landlord of The Bear. He used to exhibit his son, Thomas, later the famous painter, as artist and actor, asking his patrons, 'Gentlemen, here is my son. Will you have him recite from the poets or take your portrait?' David Garrick would retire to a summer-house in the garden to listen to young Thomas reciting poetry and Fanny Burney commented that he was 'the wonder of the family'. She described the house as being

Thomas Lawrence, father of the painter and landlord of the Bear Hotel.

The Bear Hotel and Assembly Rooms, on the site of the present Corn Exchange, in the early 1850s, and one of the earliest known photographs of Devizes.

'full of books, painting and music' and commended Thomas Lawrence senior as 'the only man on the road for warm rooms, soft beds and reading Milton'. He was also a man of some public spirit, using his own fire engine to fight town fires, sending out a posse to hunt for the notorious Poulshot highwayman Thomas Boulter and erecting 12ft-high white posts across Salisbury Plain to guide travellers to his inn in all weathers. The introduction of mail coaches in 1784, during the tenure of his successor, William Halcomb, further increased the business of The Bear, where thirty coaches stopped daily. In 1789, King George III and Queen Charlotte and a suite of forty-five halted at the inn on their way from Longleat to Savernake, at a total cost of £10 19s 0d. At the turn of the century The Bear statue was removed from its double pillar in the market place and erected over the porch of the hotel where it still sits. A few years later, new assembly rooms were built on the north side, site of the later Corn Exchange, with shops underneath and a first floor verandah from which election results were proclaimed for many years. One of these shops was used in the mid-nineteenth century as a coach office.

The high point of the coach trade was 1836, when the journey time from London had been cut to nine and a half hours at an average speed of just under 10 mph. In 1838 it was possible to travel by coach from Devizes to Birmingham in ten hours. By then, another transport system was at its peak. The Kennet and Avon Canal, constructed between 1794 and 1810, was the first artificial route made through the Pewsey Vale in modern times and greatly increased the sphere of influence of Devizes. It was also the first broad canal built to take barges carrying up to 60 tons, and had great potential for transporting agricultural produce, timber, stone, brick and coal, linking as it did with the Wiltshire and Berkshire canal at Semington and the Somerset Coal canal at Limpley Stoke. The Devizes section, which ran along the eastern limits of the old town, caused great technical difficulties, because of the steep gradients. The original route, which would have reduced the gradient and the closeness of the locks, had to be abandoned because of a local landowner's opposition. Therefore a new Bath road was constructed and the canal was taken along the route of the old road. It had to be lifted 237ft from the Avon Valley to the Vale of Pewsey by means of twenty nine locks within a distance of two and a half miles, with seventeen locks in one flight, exceeded only by the thirty locks of the Tardebigge flight on the Birmingham to Worcester canal. Three million bricks were used for the locks and the gates were made of Bowood oak. The engineer, John

A Market Place scene outside the Bear Hotel from a detail of a painting from the early nineteenth century. This building is now the National Westminster Bank.

Rennie, designed rectangular side pounds to prevent the draining of the intervening stretches when the locks were filled and Caen Hill had to be virtually reconstructed to provide a more steady incline. The deep cutting at the back of the town also caused difficulties, involving 30ft of deep digging and lining the canal with 3ft of thick puddling because of the porosity of the greensand. The excavated earth was dumped in a mound which can still be seen from Big Lane and the bottom of Dunkirk Hill. The Devizes to Foxhangers section was the last part of the canal to be completed in 1810, and a double iron railroad on wooden sleepers was constructed to haul materials up the hill. Traces of the rails are

The Caen Hill flight of locks, Kennet and Avon Canal, c. 1890.

still visible, as are the separate arches in the town bridges to accommodate the railroad.

The canal, which had cost £950,000, was open along its whole length in 1810 and the first craft navigated the locks on 28 December in three hours, carrying freestone to Savernake for the Marquis of Ailesbury. Traffic mainly consisted of Somerset coal and Devizes Wharf became a distribution depot. The Wharf Company, founded in 1807, and run eventually by the Corporation, provided weighing, cranage and warehouse facilities along the stretch from Northgate Street to Couch Lane and was a useful source of revenue to the town. John Tylee's barge of 54 tons, the King George IV, took Devizes beer to London, and West Indian tobacco was brought from Bristol for Anstie's factory. But the heyday of the canal was short. From 1841 the Great Western Railway provided a much quicker alternative method of transport and diverted the carriage of coal to the railways. Despite the application to Parliament by the canal company in 1846 for permission to build a railway along the canal bed, called 'The London, Newbury and Bath Direct Railway', GWR acquired the canal in 1852 but continued its carrying business only until 1873. The tonnage carried on the canal fell from 12,277 in 1860 to 5,372 in 1890, as the railway company allowed it to fall into disrepair. But during its prosperous years, the canal had spawned the development of the Caen Hill brickworks which flourished into the twentieth century and brought building and road making materials to Devizes to furnish its architectural and civic renewal.

BOROUGH ARMS. *PAINTED FOR THE* GUILD HALL. 1606.

The Devizes Borough Arms painted on a wooden panel in 1606 and now in the Town Hall.

St James's church and the entrance into Devizes by the London Road tollgate, from a nineteenth-century print produced by Ackermann & Co. The Green and the Crammer are in the background.

The County Courts building from a nineteenth-century Ackermann print. Today the court building awaits its fate after sitting empty for nearly two decades.

The Bath Road entrance into Devizes from a nineteenth-century Ackermann print. Trafalgar Buildings are on the left and the prison (County House of Correction) is visible in the centre background. Shane's Castle toll-house controls the gates to the Bath Road, to the left, and to Rowde, on the right.

A romantic-looking view of the Green from a nineteenth-century Ackermann print. Many of the houses in this view survive today.

An early nineteenth-century view of the Market Place from a painting in the Town Hall. The Shambles market hall, on the left, and the Market Cross were both donated by Henry Addington.

A stained glass window incorporating themes from Wiltshire's past designed by John Piper for Devizes Museum.

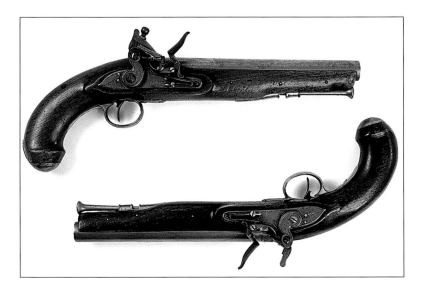

Two early nineteenth-century pistols used by warders at Devizes Prison and now in the collection at Devizes Museum.

St John's church from the Long Street entrance.

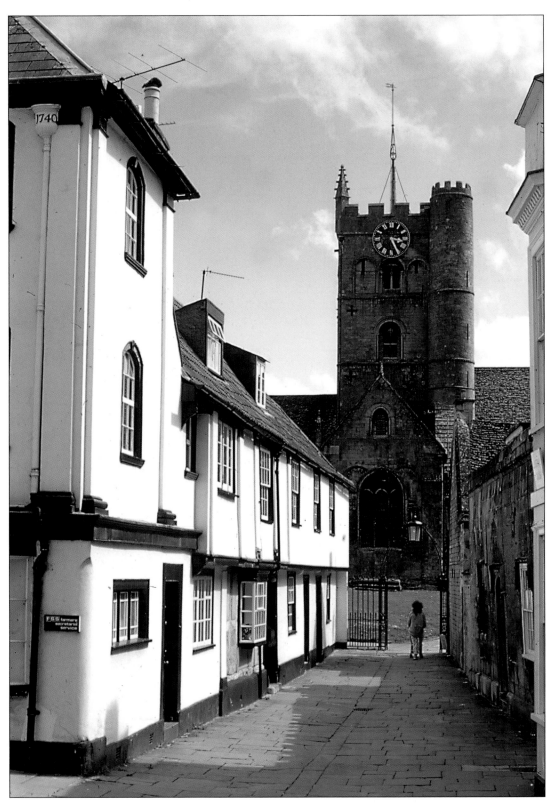

St John's Court leading to St John's church, flanked by some of the oldest dwellings in Devizes.

Devizes Wharf on the Kennet and Avon Canal with a good selection of narrow boats at mooring. The canal wharf is now a busy venue following the restoration of the Caen Hill flight and the reopening of the whole canal to traffic.

Part of the famous Caen Hill flight of locks just below the town.

St James's church seen from the Green across the Crammer.

Devizes Castle built in the mid-nineteenth century on the site of a much larger medieval castle of which almost nothing now remains. The castle is best seen in winter when there are no leaves to obscure the view.

The Escourt Fountain in the Market Place. The fountain was erected in 1879 as a memorial to Thomas Sotheron Estcourt, MP for Devizes and founder of the Wiltshire Friendly Society.

Entrance to the Bear Hotel in the Market Place decorated with summer flowers.

A Thursday market in full swing.

The formal gardens of Hillworth Park in Hillworth Road.

An aerial view of Northgate Street showing, centre, Wadworth's Northgate Brewery built in 1885. To the lower left is the brewery's original building now used as a store by Gaiger's the builders. Also visible is the Courts building, top left, and the Palace cinema, built in 1912, bottom right.

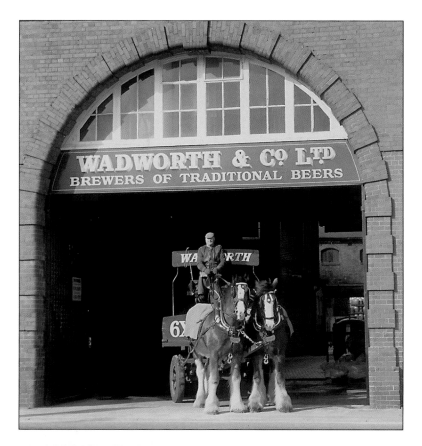

Left: *A familiar and popular sight in the town. The Wadworth's dray horses emerge from the brewery to begin another day's deliveries.*

Below: *Unpacking hops at Wadworth's brewery, now nationally famous for its traditionally-brewed 6X bitter.*

Northgate Street looking towards the Victorian Northgate Brewery and the Bath Road.

Left: *A popular Wiltshire treat is the Lardy cake. This photograph was taken in Audrey's bakery shop that used to be in the Market Place but they can still be bought elsewhere in town!*

Below: *As well as the traditional Thursday market Devizes also holds a regular Farmers' Market on the first Saturday in each month. Only goods grown or produced by the stall-holders themselves are allowed on this day.*

The Bear Hotel and the Corn Exchange decked out with flags for the annual carnival. The Corn Exchange was built in 1857 and made Devizes a market centre for corn sales. Today it is converted for a variety of social uses.

A scene from the annual carnival held for a week in late summer. In August 2000 a flock of giant birds harassed the crowds at a festival of street entertainment.

CHAPTER 8

The Nineteenth Century:
The Age of Improvement

The administrative and political reform movements of the nineteenth century had an invigorating effect on the institutions and amenities of Devizes. The Improvement Commission of 1825 made a much wider and more effective contribution to the modernizing of the town than its predecessor in 1780. Financing their expenditure from loans and rates levied on freeholders and leaseholders, the Commissioners during the next twenty years cleaned, paved and lit the town's streets. A proper road was made through the market place and the way from London Road to the top of the Brittox was reconstructed at a cost of £3,000. Streets were widened and jutting-out buildings were removed in the Brittox, Wine Street and Sidmouth Street and St John's Alley was stopped up at one end. Street name plates were erected and houses were numbered, the first number in each street beginning at the point nearest the market-place on the left-hand side of the street. Trees in front of houses were removed and no thatch was to be used or repaired. Projecting water spouts were replaced by wall pipes and all doors and gates were to open inwards. Under the streets drainage culverts were laid, leading into the sewers, the streets were swept three times a week and the keeping of pigs in the town was banned. Detailed arrangements were made for fire-fighting procedures, with the canal company providing water for a reservoir in the market place; all fire-fighting equipment, including the new fire engine bought in London, was kept in the Shambles. Devizes was one of the first towns in the country to be lit by gas and four night-watchmen and a night constable were appointed in 1835 to patrol the streets, armed with lanthorns, staves and rattles and with power to challenge 'all suspicious persons'. The public houses were to close at 10 p.m., 'the Committee having the fullest conviction that much mischief arises from the conduct of persons, who, under the influence of strong drink, go wandering about at a late hour'. In 1848 the borough police, based in the old Bridewell, were incorporated into the County Constabulary.

Devizes Market Place around 1860, from a lithograph by E. Buckler.

By now Devizes had a new prison in the Bath Road, described by William Cobbett as a 'monstrous building'. Built at a cost of some £30,000 on a polygonal plan with the Governor's house in the centre, the 'new Bridewell' as it was at first called, contained 210 cells and had a staff of ten. Overcrowding and a diet of bread and gruel together with long hours spent on the treadmill led to a mutiny in 1822, which was quelled with the help of 200 local tradesmen sworn in as special constables. The régime remained grim, however, with strict rules of silence, solitary confinement for those unable to work and flogging or consignment to 'the dark cells' for such offences as turning the head when working on the treadmill. Even the design of the weather vane incorporated leg irons and a key. Of the two hundred prisoners in 1827, ninety-four were convicted of poaching and forty-six of vagrancy; as the chaplain rightly pointed out, the lack of segregation of prisoners was in effect 'a step to the gallows'. Those condemned to die were allowed to attend service in the chapel on the Sunday before, with their coffins open in front of them. Between 1824 and 1860 executions were held in public on top of the lodge at the prison entrance and many thousands flocked to watch. The execution of Rebecca Smith in 1849 for the murder of her infant child by rat poison attracted a crowd of around thirty thousand people. A fly boat even ran a special trip along the canal from Pewsey. Opportunistic traders sold ballad sheets to the spectators, such as:

> At eight o'clock on Monday morn
> Charles Gerrish crossed the river
> No more he'll cuss the income tax
> Nor grumble at his liver

Gerrish, a workhouse pauper, had murdered a fellow inmate by thrusting a red hot poker into his neck. The last execution took place in 1903. During the First World War the prison was used as a military detention barracks, and it was demolished between 1924 and 1927.

The social distress after the Napoleonic Wars led to a revival of radical agitation for parliamentary reform, and there were disturbances in London and the north of England, to which the Home Secretary and former Devizes MP, Lord Sidmouth, responded by a policy of repression. In 1817 the Sheriff of Wiltshire called a meeting in Devizes market place to organize an address to the Prince Regent, congratulating him on his escape from harm during a demonstration on his return from opening Parliament. 'Orator' Henry Hunt, a leading radical and Wiltshire farmer, tried to address the meeting but was mobbed by bellowing and braying local Tories, and, in his words, 'but for the impenetrable phalanx of gallant, brave and kind-hearted Wiltshiremen, who formed with their persons an impregnable bulwark to all the assaults of constables, bullies and blackguards, urged on by the Mayor, the consequences might have proved very serious'. With some difficulty, he was borne off on the shoulders of his supporters to the safety of the Castle Inn.

The Mayor and Corporation were implacably opposed to the notion of parliamentary reform that might erode their electoral privileges, but the present system was patently unfair. The Council of thirty-five, of whom fifteen were non-resident, elected the

The gate of the County House of Correction on the top of which executions took place. The prison was demolished in the mid-1920s.

town's two MPs. The highest number who had ever voted was thirty in 1830. The Corporation claimed that Devizes had never been guilty of bribery and corruption, and emphasized the importance of retaining the link between property and representation. The agricultural riots in 1830 had caused great alarm among the landowners, and the stock of gunpowder, kept by Burt's the ironmongers, had been buried for safety. In the eyes of the Corporation, reform was equated with revolution. But a growing local agitation in favour of reform was led by tradesmen, professionals and Nonconformists, notably Wadham Locke, Dr Brabant, Robert Waylen and Benjamin and Paul Anstie, with meetings, petitions and letters to the Press. When the Reform Act was finally passed in 1832 a great festival was held on the Green, with a procession of 1,600 people, dinner and fireworks. The Act made Devizes the election town of the northern division of the county; it retained its two MPs, but the franchise was extended to male householders paying £10 annual rent, an increase of over four hundred. In 1867, by the second Reform Act, Devizes lost one of its MPs, and the right to vote was extended to working class males, increasing the electorate to about a thousand - despite the dire warning from the Conservative MP for Devizes, Thomas Bateson, that it would 'Americanize the English Constitution'.

The Municipal Corporations Act of 1835 continued the reforming process. The Council was to be elected by all male ratepayers; the town was divided into north and south wards, each with nine councillors, three to be elected annually; six aldermen, three from each ward, would be elected by the Council for six years, and the mayor annually. The new Council's first action was to appoint a Finance Committee. Their report in 1836 on the previous fifty years revealed a state of extravagance, slackness and mismanagement. No proper records had been kept of leases, debts and contracts. Excessive expenditure on addresses to the King, lavish payments on beer for Constables, workmen and recruiting parties, unexplained legal expenses, election dinners at £100 a time, and extravagances such as £9 17s 6d for gold tassels for cushions on the mayor's seat in St Mary's, had combined to produce a debt of £4,667. The Finance Committee proposed to tackle the problem by increasing rents, selling property, and more efficient toll collection. The Council pursued its new open policy by publishing its accounts and admitting reporters to its meetings.

Devizes had acquired a newspaper in 1819, when George Simpson moved his *Simpson's Salisbury Journal* to Devizes, renaming it the *Devizes and Wiltshire Gazette*, which was to remain in the family's hands for three generations. Other nineteenth-century newspapers included the *Wiltshire Independent*, the mouthpiece of Liberalism in the town, which amalgamated with the *Wiltshire Times* in 1876, and the *Devizes Advertiser*, started by Charles Gillman in 1858, which used the first gas-operated printing press in the district in 1877.

Six daily newspapers were taken by the Literary and Scientific Institute established in 1833 in Northgate Street. It ran a library and museum, and held lectures on scientific subjects; its rules specified that the management committee must include some 'journeymen mechanics'. The Mechanics' Institute in the High Street also provided popular lectures, and a Working Men's Reading Room was opened in the Little Brittox in 1856. By now the seventeenth- and eighteenth-century town charity schools had been supplemented by Anglican and Nonconformist establishments run by the National Society and the British and Foreign Schools Society and a large number of privately run day and boarding schools, foremost of which was the Revd Mr Pugh's Grammar School at Heathcote House. The Grange in Bridewell Street housed a charitable infant day nursery, where working class women could leave their children from 8 a.m. to 6 p.m.

Although many women supplemented their husbands' wages by dressmaking or taking in washing, most single women worked as shop assistants, domestic servants or factory hands. The 1891 census for St James's parish alone records fifty-five domestic

The Ansties' building in the Market Place, built in 1894, decorated for the Coronation of Queen Elizabeth II in 1953

Brown and May's foundry in Estcourt Street, in the early years of the twentieth century.

servants. There were many small general shops in Devizes at this time; an 1894 directory lists thirty-six grocers and general stores, fifteen bakers and confectioners and seven drapers. Many women worked as tobacco packers at Ansties' factory, which had acquired a 10 hp Boulton and Watt steam engine in 1831, at the same time enlarging its premises. New firms established in Devizes in the nineteenth century widened the choice of jobs for men. William Brown and Charles May, who began trading in 1854 at the Estcourt Street foundry, gained worldwide renown for their traction engines, threshing engines and motor tractors. T.H. White grew out of an ironmongery shop in the Brittox. From producing dairy utensils and wagon wheels, the business became one of the leading firms of agricultural engineers, making new machinery, such as elevators, winnowing machines and chaff cutters and gaining contracts from all over the world, even supplying the Egyptian Government with irrigation machines. In 1901 it employed 350 workers.

The Devizes Brick and Tile Company at Caen Hill developed after excavations for the canal revealed the largest exposure of Gault and lower greensand clays in Wiltshire. At its peak, it employed forty men with an annual output of two-and-a-half million bricks from four kilns. Devizes bricks were used in the new Ansties' offices erected in the market place in 1894, Pans Lane villas, the large houses on the Potterne Road and Roundway Hospital chapel. The brickworks closed in 1961. Wadworth's Brewery, designed by Henry Wadworth and built in 1885 by direct labour, dominates the northern end of the market place. Ten years before, Henry Wadworth had bought the Northgate Brewery, now part of Gaigers' premises and formerly Robert Waylen's cloth factory, and in 1889 the firm amalgamated with Humby's Brewery of Estcourt Street. By 1900 it had over thirty freehold inns in the district and stabled fifty delivery horses. But alongside all these large enterprises there were still many small firms, saddlers, coach-builders, carpenters, plumbers and coal merchants, employing apprentices. Most boys leaving school at twelve would make a start by becoming an apprentice or an errand boy. Another opening was that of clerk to the increasing number of insurance firms, solicitors, auctioneers and accountants who were becoming established in the town, a further sign of growing prosperity.

Both Devizes traders and the Council were aware of the economic importance of a railway to an 'Assize town and the principal market town in the county of Wiltshire'. A single line track to Melksham from near Dunkirk Hill was proposed in 1836 to link with Bath, Bristol, Chippenham and Reading and so facilitate wider distribution of agricultural produce but the plan came to nothing. Five years later, because of the technical difficulties of a 1 in 52 gradient up Caen Hill, Brunel recommended the Swindon-Chippenham main line route to the west rather than Devizes and Bradford-on-Avon. There was also much opposition from landowners, who thought that the advantages of a railway were 'doubtful ... Devizes not being a manufacturing town' and, more significantly, that there would be

Devizes Station in the 1950s.

'injury to Private Property of great magnitude'. But supporters of the railway persisted and in 1856, by means of petitions and public meetings, succeeded in getting the Wiltshire, Somerset and Weymouth Railway to extend a single line broad gauge track from Holt Junction to Devizes, with the station sunk deeply into the escarpment. The first service train in 1857 arrived to the strains of 'Hail the Conquering Hero Comes', and the first excursion to Weymouth conveyed 1,000 passengers in twenty-three carriages. Not until 1862 did Devizes acquire a link with London. A petition to the GWR emphasized the importance of Devizes as the county town of north Wiltshire, the centre of a large agricultural district, with one of the largest weekly corn markets in the west of England. The major difficulty involved in the Berkshire and Hampshire extension line from Hungerford, opened on 11 November 1862, was the 190-yard tunnel under Devizes castle, with foundations 20 to 30 ft below the level of the old moat.

The period 1862-99 marked the maximum sphere of economic influence for Devizes, when it was on the semi-main line route through the Pewsey Vale; but with the construction of the Westbury line through Lavington in 1900 Devizes was again bypassed. The railway brought tangible benefits to the town. It confirmed the status of Devizes as the market centre of a wide area; special market day tickets were issued within a 20-mile radius. It facilitated recreational travel for many villagers who had rarely left their own areas; in May 1893 some six thousand people came by rail to see the Royal Wiltshire Yeomanry's centenary celebrations,

Carriers' carts in the Market Place in the 1880s.

Firework display on The Green to celebrate the abolition of the turnpike gates in 1868.

which were visited by the Prince of Wales. Local firms could send their produce, meat, agricultural produce, milk and tobacco, in bulk to London and building materials could be more easily and quickly transported. The establishment of a coal depôt at the station increased the number of coal merchants in the town; in 1894 there were seven. It also provided fuel for domestic use, the local gasworks and for powering the steam engines of the town's industries.

But the railway killed off the canal and long distance coach routes. In 1889 there were only two coaches running through Devizes, from Bath to Southampton and Bath to Hungerford. It did, however, stimulate the local trade of carriers, who advertised their services as feeders to the railway. In 1850, before Devizes acquired its own railway, a service ran from the Crown Hotel to Chippenham five times a day, to enable passengers to catch trains to London, Bath and Bristol. Carriers started from inns such as The Bear, The Crown and The Swan, to the great profit of local innkeepers. In the period 1883-6 forty-three carriers were working on routes to Devizes, mostly on market day, within a radius of Marlborough, Warminster and Salisbury, and this carrying trade is a good indicator of the town's economic hinterland. Many of the carriers easily adapted to motor bus transport in the twentieth century and a few continued in business until the Second World War.

Travel was no longer delayed by stoppages at turnpike gates, which were abolished in 1868. On the last day of tolls a band processed to all the gates in Devizes, playing various airs and the national anthem. The gates were hauled around the town in a

The Market Cross showing the posts and rails against which farmers placed sacks of corn for sale in the days before the Corn Exchange. Photograph by John Chivers, 1890s.

wagon decorated with flags and evergreens, and then burnt on a bonfire on Etchilhampton Hill, the blaze being visible throughout the Pewsey Vale. A week later Professor Gyngell from Wells gave a firework display on the Green, concluding with a 16ft long design of a turnpike gate, which was destroyed by cannon, and surmounted by the motto 'Missed but not wanted'.

New landmarks were appearing around Devizes. As early as 1837, 178 farmers and dealers had petitioned for a covered corn market to protect their produce, which had for many years been stacked against two semi-circles of railings in the centre of the market place. Such a building, they thought, would 'tend to increase the Trade of the town at large'. Twenty years later a new Corn Exchange was erected on the site of the Bear Assembly Rooms, which were moved to the Bear yard. William Hill, architect of Portsmouth Guildhall, was chosen from sixty applicants and the building work was done by a local firm, J. Randell. Difficulties were encountered in the construction work because of the proximity of wells and the town ditch , but the florid Victorian building was finally opened on 3 December 1857, surmounted by the statue of Ceres, Roman goddess of harvest, presented by the local MP, Christopher Darby-Griffith. The cost of £3,500 had largely been borne by gifts and local subscriptions. A novel feature of the opening dinner, attended by 340 and entertained by a Hanoverian band, was the presence of ladies, which a local newspaper thought 'not desirable'. The new building greatly increased the trade and prestige of the market; in 1889 dealers came from as far afield as Bristol, Uxbridge and Cardiff.

The market place gained another feature in 1879 when the fountain was erected by subscription in memory of Thomas Sotheron Estcourt, MP for Devizes, Marlborough and north Wiltshire, at various times. He is best remembered as the founder of the Wiltshire Friendly Society in 1828, which was later housed in the Jacobean-style building at the bottom of Long Street. Piped water was still something of a novelty, and special trains brought in over 2,000 people to the fountain opening ceremony, which, although initially marred by the failure of the cord to open the curtain, subsequently turned out to be a successful event. There was a dinner in the Corn Exchange for 800 and at dusk the fountain was illuminated with 'parabolic' gas lighting. A subscription by 600 persons had earlier raised nearly all the money needed for the building of the Assize Court in Northgate Street in 1835. Designed in Bath stone in classical style by T.H. Wyatt, it provided a prestige setting for the annual Assizes, the Quarter Sessions and the Borough and Magistrates' Courts. In 1868 the Council bought Northgate House opposite the former King's Arms, for the judge's lodgings, and until 1971 the judge's colourful procession across the road to court was a regular feature of the calendar.

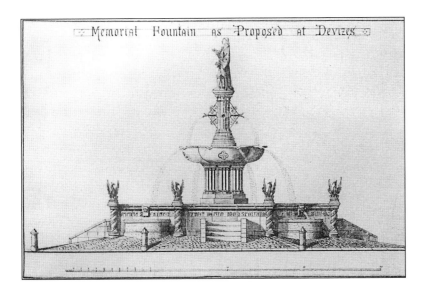

Design for the fountain erected in 1879 in the Market Place to commemorate Thomas Sotheron Estcourt.

Devizes Cottage Hospital, opened in 1872.

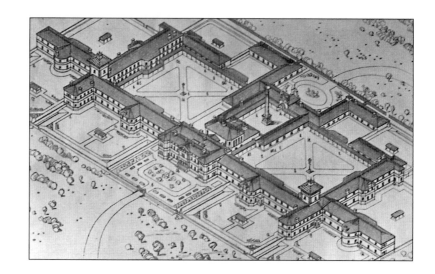

Plan of the Wiltshire County Asylum, later Roundway Hospital, opened in 1851.

Aerial view showing the extensive site of the County Asylum, closed in 1995.

The Asylum was also designed by T.H. Wyatt, but in the Italian style 'as the simplest, the lightest and most cheerful'. It absorbed patients from former private asylums at Dunkirk Hill, New Park Street and Belle Vue. The régime of the first Superintendent, John Thurnam, the craniologist, was kind and enlightened; he even employed some of the inmates on his private archaeological digs. But later visitors reported overcrowding and excessive economy. It became a local joke that Devizes possessed the county gaol, the county lunatic asylum and the county police station. Devizes had become the home of the first county police force in the country, established in 1839, as well as being the base for the Wiltshire Regiment in 1878 when Le Marchant Barracks were built on the London Road, the mayor and some councillors having waited on Edward Cardwell, the Secretary of State for War, to press the claims of Devizes to be an army centre. Its castellated appearance was appropriate, not only militarily but also historically. By now Devizes had acquired a new castle, built and embellished over a period of forty years by Valentine Leach, a local draper, and his son Robert, in a strange mixture of Norman and Gothic styles. A later owner, Sir Charles Rich, made further alterations and added Tudor-style windows.

With its new public buildings and county-wide organizations, Devizes was now the second town in Wiltshire. Because of increased employment opportunities its population doubled in the course of the nineteenth century, from 3,547 to 6,532, and there was much housing expansion along Northgate Street, Bath Road, London Road, Rotherstone and Southgate, and on land formerly occupied by stables and coach yards. Between 1816 and 1836 about three hundred houses were built, some by Captain Needham

Devizes castle in the early part of the twentieth century.

A castle interior showing elaborate Victorian ornamentation and fittings.

Long Street around the turn of the twentieth century.

Taylor, who was responsible for the construction of Trafalgar Place, Southgate House and four shops at the south-east end of the Brittox. Here larger shop windows were replacing the former small panes of glass, and in the market place and Station Road trees were planted. The Shambles were rebuilt and extended in 1838 and Devizes acquired a hospital, sewage and waterworks, cemetery, fire brigade and public bathrooms in the market place. The first commercial telephone to be used for practical purposes in England was assembled by Alfred Cunnington in 1878, connecting his home at Southgate House with his business in the Old Town Hall. To the nineteenth-century inhabitant the pace of change and progress must have seemed remarkable. And yet he could still enjoy the circuses and dancing bears, the Devizes Stakes, cricket matches and picnics on Roundway Down, and Tan Hill Fair in August, the origins of which stretched far beyond the history of Devizes itself.

Map of Devizes showing outward expansion of the town, c. 1835.

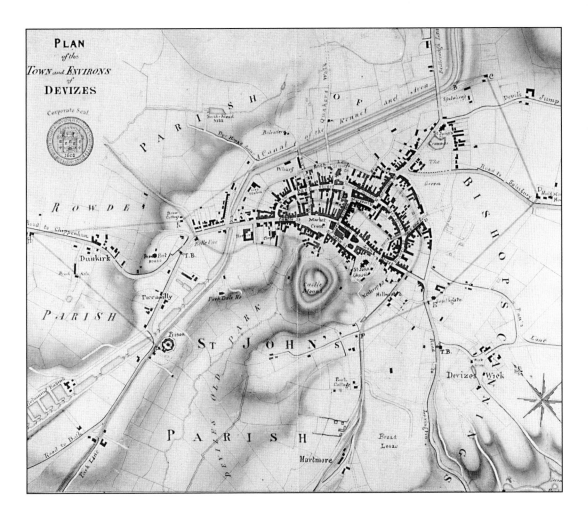

CHAPTER 9

The Twentieth Century:
Continuity and Change

In the 1920s and early 1930s it would have been possible to travel to Tan Hill Fair by car or bus. Dr Henry Mackay of Lansdowne House was the first person in Devizes to acquire a car licence, for his 8hp green Dennis with yellow wheels, in 1903. In the next few years, he was followed by other leading townsmen, such as G.E. Anstie, Marler Sloper, William Henry Brown and Edward Colston of Roundway Park. Some of the earliest cars belonged to the proprietor of The Bear Hotel and the owners of the new garages that had sprung up, run by Samuel Henry Ward, later to become Ward's Motors, and Willis's, the coachbuilders, now adapting to the new form of transport.

The earliest trade van was Sloper's in red and green. The Chief Constable's car was unmistakable, in pansy purple with white lines, a hood and brass fittings. The more adventurous were buying motorcycles from about 1903 and soon the newspapers were reporting the first fatal accident, at Stert in 1907. Motor charabancs provided a new mode of transport for outings and buses slowly began to replace the carriers' carts, though in 1918 there were still twenty-four carts to twenty-one buses serving the villages. In the 1930s Cinderella Bull still ran her pony and trap from Rowde to Devizes on market days. One carrier, Munday, at the Pelican, survived until 1939, running his service to Potterne, Lavington and Tilshead. In 1888, the White Lion had advertised accommodation for horses; in 1924, the Royal Oak publicized car parking in its yard. In 1927 there was still a bath chair proprietor in Bridewell Street, but the Bear garage was running a motor omnibus to meet every train.

In the 1920s and 1930s, however, much traffic was still horse-drawn. Coal merchants, brewers, milkmen and bakers all used horse and cart for deliveries and the Corporation dust cart and water cart to lay the dust in hot weather were familiar sights. Most workmen cycled; even builders might be seen carrying a precariously balanced bucket on the handlebars and a ladder on one shoulder. Carts and waggons still lumbered up to Roundway

Shane's Castle, Bath Road, early twentieth century.

Hill, after 1930 the property of the Corporation, with excited schoolchildren for tea, games and races.

The highlight of the year for many was the annual Sunday School outing to Weymouth. A public bathing place had been created in 1878 at the second canal pound below the town, and was in use from May till October, until a new swimming pool opened in 1936 in Colston Road. Whist drives, fêtes, rifle shooting, and concerts at the Oddfellows' Hall in Maryport Street enlivened the monotony of work.

But the greatest wonder was the New Electric Theatre, opened in the market place in 1912 and built by Chivers. Its décor was striking - niches with figures bearing electric light torches, a balcony panelled with flowers and leaves in pink, green and gold, and busts of writers including Shakespeare on the walls. Furnished with plush leather tip seats, it had a sloping floor so that all could get a good view 'provided the ladies will remove their hats'. Such was the sense of momentous progress that the Mayor and Corporation attended the opening performance to witness 'the excellent programme of photoplays'. Another sensation was provided by Sir Alan Cobham's Flying Circus, where biplanes flew under the branches of tall trees and picked up handkerchiefs from the ground with a hook on the wing tip. Gazette readers were offered twelve free flights at Rowdefield Farm in April 1934. In the early 1920s Devizes even had a wireless station on the golf course, with 300ft-tall masts that handled radio signals for North Atlantic shipping. Electricity was still rare. Ansties', Chivers, the Palace Cinema and Roundway House had their own generators, but Devizes railway station did not have electricity right up to the time it closed in 1966.

Despite the technical advances Devizes still had one foot in the nineteenth century. There were still many small shops and sweet shops in converted front rooms. The muffin man stood in the Little Brittox with a basket on his head, ringing his handbell. Cracked eggs could be bought cheaply from the Egg Dépot in Monday Market Street and Hampton's Dairy in Long Street sold milk at a discount to be collected in a jug in the side yard. Hampton's had its own dairy herds and Jump Farm supplied Guernsey milk daily. Rose's, the butchers in Sidmouth Street, ran its own grazing farm of 130 acres and five slaughter houses still existed in the town in the early twentieth century. Cattle were sold on the hoof on market day, with calves in pens, and hens, rabbits and ferrets in coops round the market cross. Stalls in the market sold cockles and mussels and a little further away, in New Park Street, an early form of twentieth-century 'take-away' sold tripe, chitterlings, faggots

Aerial view of the north end of town in 1924 showing the canal, the canal swimming pool and the prison, shortly before demolition.

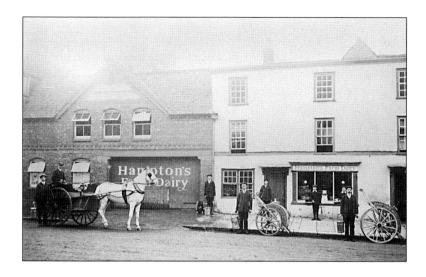

Hampton's Dairy in
Long Street, c. 1910.

The Palace cinema
opened in 1912.

Palace cinema
programme for 1921.

and peas. There was even an itinerant dentist working on a platform near the Market Cross, employing a boy to beat a drum to mask the cries of his victims. The cheapness of public transport, with railway stations in many villages, drew shoppers to Devizes on market days from a wide area.

This was still the age of the family department store. Charles Sloper's in the Brittox, with its arcade and overhead rail cash system, traded on four floors. Growing out of a business founded by Joseph Sloper in 1832, it had gradually extended its premises and stock, adding furniture, dressmaking and removals, and a toy bazaar in the basement, visited every December by Father Christmas, who arrived by train and cart rather than by reindeer. During the horse fairs in spring and autumn, travel-weary shoppers were given free refreshments. Marler Sloper's in Maryport Street, Clappen's in Wine Street and Kemp's in the Brittox were gentlemen's outfitters still catering for a formal style of dressing. The International was the first multiple store in Devizes, opening in 1889 as The Indian Empire Tea Company. The Co-op started as a small shop in Maryport Street in 1898, moving a few months later to 40 New Park Street and transporting its stock on a pair of trucks. In 1899 it traded at 56 Northgate Street, using No. 57 as a tea-room and the infants' schoolroom at the rear as a bake-house. The move to the Market Place at the top of Snuff Street in 1936 introduced the one jarring architectural note in a space otherwise retaining its Georgian style.

But continuity and change were the twin themes of the twentieth century. During the period between the two world wars, industries appropriate to an agricultural district flourished in the town. The Central Wilts Bacon Company, established in 1899,

Willis's carriage builders on the corner of Snuff Street, c. 1900.

The Brittox with Charles Sloper's department store (centre), Sawyers leather shop (right) and, opposite, Marler Sloper's outfitters (left).

took 90 per cent of its pigs from within a 20-mile radius of Devizes. Its production rate of fifty pigs a week in 1900 rose to 240 a week in 1937. After a wartime interval when its premises were used for Government food storage it was handling 1,000 pigs a week in 1950, and had shops in the Little Brittox and Maryport Street. But cheap imports began to affect its trade and when it closed in 1960 its premises were taken over by a light engineering firm from Bath, Cross Manufacturing. The North Wilts Dairy established in 1889 in Estcourt Street later moved to Pans Lane, where it specialized in soft cheeses, processing the milk of 1,200 cows. A flax industry became established in London Road during the Second World

*Devizes horse fair on
The Green, 1930s.*

War, employing 180 workers and making fibre for tents and parachute harnesses. Seventy-two Wiltshire farmers came to include flax in their rotation system and the aroma of the flax factory became a familiar feature of Devizes streets, along with the smell of hops from the brewery. The war also boosted T.H. White's agricultural engineering business. The shortage of labour on the farms and the need to produce more food increased the demand for the supply and maintenance of farm machinery.

It was in the twentieth century that building and construction, emerging from small beginnings in the previous century, became one of the major industries of the town, employing 30 per cent of all male workers. William Rendell, an ironmonger and white-smith, came to Devizes from Devon in 1840; his first job was to fix the railings around the new Assize Court. In 1858 he sold his ironmongery business to Joseph Burt to concentrate on building work and the firm expanded rapidly in the twentieth century. Chivers began as a one-man carpentry and joinery shop in a room over stables at the Rising Sun in 1883, William Edward Chivers' first task being to make a serving hatch at the Tap, later the Volunteer Arms, in Southbroom Road. He walked twelve miles to Honeystreet to order £16-worth of timber as he could not afford the rail fare. In 1911 the firm expanded into building work, its first contract being two cottages in Pans Lane. When Brown and May closed in the following year, Chivers moved to the foundry in Estcourt Street. During the First World War the firm was awarded Government building contracts, also furnishing steam lorries to

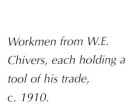

Workmen from W.E. Chivers, each holding a tool of his trade, c. 1910.

transport troops and munitions. In the Second World War Chivers constructed military camps and aerodromes and after 1945 became renowned for work on the Atomic Energy Establishments at Harwell and Aldermaston. The Estcourt offices were rebuilt in 1965 and by 1970 Chivers employed 1,500 people, a quarter of them in Devizes, and had become one of the biggest building firms in the country; its closure in 1985 was a great economic shock to the town. Other family building businesses included Offer's, Maslen's, and Gaiger Brothers, the last named being responsible for many of the town's public buildings and housing estates.

Some old industries disappeared in the twentieth century. Ansties' had continued to expand its production of a wide range of cigarettes and tobacco, such as 'On Furlough', 'Daydreams', 'Black Beauty' and Farmer's Glory' until the sale of the business to the Imperial Tobacco Company in 1944 ended six generations of

Rendell's builders lorry.

family control. In 1961 the firm ceased to trade but the closure of Ansties', Brown and May, the Central Wilts Bacon Company and Stratton's the wholesale grocers based in Monday Market Street, had a less serious effect on the local economy than had been feared. New light industries appeared in the town to absorb some of the unemployed. In the electronics field, Savages moved from London in 1940 and later transferred the whole business, which manufactured transformers and electrical equipment. Hinchleys took over the old Wilts United Dairies factory in Pans Lane in 1949, making electrical components for radio and electrical firms and the Ministry of Supply. By 1952 its workforce had risen from 67 to 250, providing a useful source of employment for women, while the presence of military establishments on the outskirts of the town and on Salisbury Plain also stimulated the growth of the commercial side of the town's economy.

The Second World War in many ways marks a watershed in the twentieth-century history of Devizes. The influx of about a thousand evacuees from London, and the presence of Canadian, Australian and American troops widened the horizons of Devizes folk. Local men and women serving in the forces married out of the town and moved away after the war, while increasing mobility brought new employment and living patterns. The post-war baby boom created housing needs which led to the expansion of the

Tobacco sorting room at Anstie's factory, around 1920.

Devizes market in the 1920s.

town's residential areas and the consequent prosperity of the building trade. The break up of landed estates at the turn of the century had already started this process. In 1899 the sale of the Estcourt estate, the last great landholding in Devizes, freed building land in the Nursteed Road, Wick Lane and Pans Lane areas and the Council had taken the opportunity of acquiring the Green and the Crammer. The demolition of the prison allowed building to take place in the Bath Road area and in the 1930s the Council embarked on a process of slum clearance of courts and alleys, the result of eighteenth- and nineteenth-century in-filling, such as Hare and Hounds Court, Cross Keys Yard and part of Gains Lane. It was calculated that a fifth of the town's houses were slums. An increase in the town's population to 7,897 by 1951 made the problem urgent and during the period 1945-58 twice the number of houses were built as in the inter-war years, mainly in the Hillworth and Brickley Lane areas, with a further programme of slum clearance in New Park Street and The Nursery. The extent of pre-war overcrowding is demonstrated by the fact that the multi-storey flats built in Sheep Street in the 1950s only accommodated half the number of people previously living in the old courts and cottages. In the 1970s and '80s, housing associations also provided accommodation, and further council estates were built at Mayenne Place and Waiblingen Way, with private estates in the Broadleas and Roundway areas and in the 1990s the town has greatly expanded on its eastern side.

Estcourt Street and Sidmouth Street junction, c. 1900.

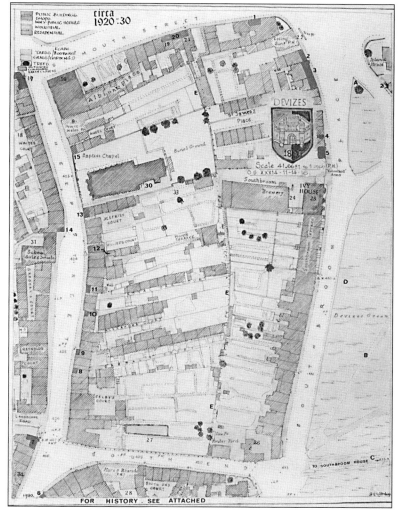

Plan of the Sheep Street courts and cottages, 1920-30.

The Brittox in the 1950s.

Imaginative restoration schemes in Hare and Hounds Street and Wharfside have both won national awards.

The post-war Council had ambitious plans, which included a bypass and an improved rail service, though they did not implement suggestions made in the 1930s that the market place should be moved to the Wharf or that a municipal airport should be built on the London Road. The idea of acquiring the castle was rejected, though the purchase of Hillworth Park has provided an attractive recreational area. Public reaction to the proposed demolition of Great Porch House in advance of a link road and to the building of a brick wall around the Crammer pond led to the formation of the Trust for Devizes, a civic conservation body that has done much to protect the character and amenities of the town from unsympathetic development. Devizes has acquired some modern public buildings, such as the police headquarters, police station, fire station, leisure centre, Devizes school and a public library. New industrial estates are growing on the edges of the town but Devizes lacks the ideal communications necessary to attract industry on a large scale.

The fact that Devizes lies in the centre of Wiltshire and is the home to so many county organizations created the expectation that it would become the county town. Indeed it was decided in May 1930 that the new county headquarters should be built at Southbroom, and Pans Lane Halt was created with that in mind. But in 1934 the County Council was offered a site in Trowbridge free of cost. The lack of a good railway service was a factor counting against Devizes, since County Council regulations stipulated that wherever possible, journeys should be made by bus or train. With the reorganization of local government in 1974

Devizes lost its borough status, but became the headquarters of Kennet District Council, which moved from Northgate House to Browfort in 1979. The main problem facing Devizes in the last twenty years has been to reconcile the preservation of the historic core of the town with the demands of increased traffic and changes in shopping patterns. The disc parking scheme, one way streets, the link road and the pedestrianisation of the Brittox all helped to alleviate congestion in some of the narrower streets, although excessive house building on the town's outskirts threatens to cause further traffic problems.

Devizes has a large rural catchment area for shopping and employment. Twenty-five thousand people live within a five mile radius of the town centre, with fifty villages within ten miles. Devizes has come to owe its prosperity to the surrounding district, acting as a magnet particularly at the end of the Pewsey Vale. A Board of Trade survey in 1961 reported that Devizes shops produced £2.9 million in retail sales annually. There is a wider range of shops than in many towns of similar size, and the compactness of the retail centre makes shopping easy. Of the Wiltshire towns only Devizes, Salisbury and Marlborough, with their wide market places, have preserved a market atmosphere. Lacking water power and inorganic raw materials, Devizes has escaped the impact of industrial development and heavy industry has never been so important to Devizes as to Trowbridge, Melksham or Bradford-on-Avon. Its most successful modern industrial activities have been closely associated with agriculture, such as bacon, milk, cheese, brewing and traction engines.

The growth of Devizes has been limited by the high quality of the surrounding farmland and the steep fall away of land around the town, which creates natural boundaries to the south and west. Throughout its history Devizes has remained closely allied with the land, and remains an unspoilt market town. The pleasant settings of the Green, the Crammer, the castle and the market place and the architectural beauty of its fine churches and Georgian buildings give it a certain tourist potential. It has over 200 Grade I and Grade II listed buildings in the town centre; only eighteen towns in Britain have more. But Devizes has managed to achieve a balance between self-conscious tourist appeal and the practicalities of everyday commercial and residential life. Many events and personalities have moulded its development and left behind visual reminders of the past, but Devizes has mellowed over a thousand years; from royal castle and cloth town, it has now returned to its origins as a market town and, as the proverb has it, 'the market is the best garden'.

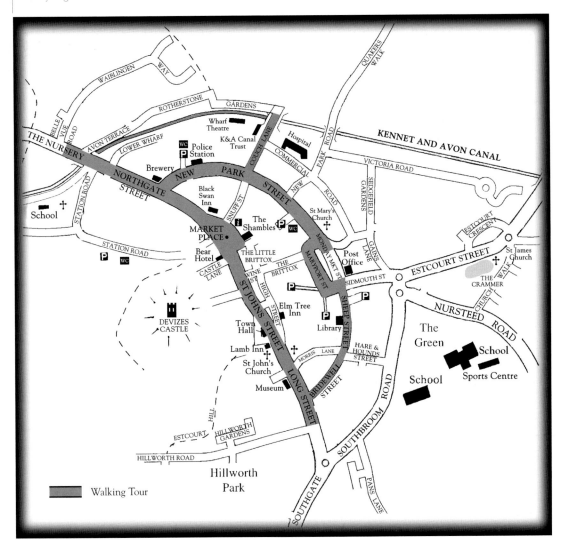

Street plan of Devizes town centre.

WALKING TOUR

The walk begins in Devizes Market Place and largely follows the medieval street pattern of the town, which is one of the best preserved in Britain. If time allows, the tour can be extended to take in the Crammer, St James's church and the Green, and also Hillworth Park. Wheelchair users should be able to follow the route without difficulty, though care needs to be taken crossing the busy A361 road and pedestrian crossings should be used wherever possible, even if this means a slight detour.

Start by walking into the middle of Devizes Market Place to the market cross.

The market place, one of the largest in the west of England, is a mixture of civic and commercial buildings, inns and fine eighteenth-century houses. When John Leland in 1545 declared that the beauty of Devizes was 'all in one street', he was referring to the market place, laid out in the fifteenth century as the townspeople encroached on the castle's outer defences. It is funnel-shaped, and you are now standing in the widest part.

The first market cross, which was near the entrance to St John's Street just past The Bear, was pulled down in 1806. Until the first years of the nineteenth century, there stood near the site of the present market cross a double column of pillars surmounted by the black bear which is now over the porch of The Bear Hotel; the

Devizes Market Place in 1798 from a painting by Robert Noyes. The Bear statue rests atop two columns and the original market cross is to its left.

pillars are now in the hotel yard. The western side of the market cross where you are standing records that it was the gift of Henry Addington, Viscount Sidmouth, former MP for Devizes, who was Home Secretary for ten years and Prime Minister for three. On the eastern side, a panel incorporates the story of Ruth Pierce, a woman from nearby Potterne, who dropped down dead in the market place in 1753, after having sworn that she had paid her share in a wheat transaction in the market. The cross, made of Bath stone and dating from 1814, is fashioned in Georgian Gothic style, and was designed by Benjamin Wyatt, son of the architect. Originally it was surrounded by a double circle of railings against which farmers used to stack their sacks of corn on market days until the building of the Corn Exchange in 1857. The cross now provides a focal point for processions and civic occasions.

Turn now to face the western side of the market place.

Here stands The Bear Hotel. dating at least from the sixteenth century. As the coach trade increased in the late eighteenth century, the older part was given a stucco front, a Doric porch and bay windows and an extension was built, with a Bath stone façade, Ionic pilasters and a wrought iron verandah, on the south side on the site of stables belonging to The White Hart at the corner of Castle Lane. On the north side stood a late eighteenth-century Assembly Room with large sash windows, which was removed to The Bear yard when the Corn Exchange was built and now houses the hotel ballroom . This assembly room also had a verandah and shops on the ground floor. Behind The Bear were ornamental gardens, now part of the castle grounds, and the extensive stables stretched to behind The Pelican inn. In its eighteenth-century heyday, The Bear was visited by royalty and literary and artistic figures and was the home of young Thomas Lawrence, later the portrait painter, whose father was landlord for seven years. It was also a centre for the town's social and philanthropic activities.

Next to The Bear is the Corn Exchange, built in 1857 in Victorian 'classical' style of Bath stone, more readily available since the opening of the Kennet and Avon Canal in 1810. The building, with its Corinthian columns, stone balustrade and relief carvings, is surmounted by the statue of Ceres, the Roman goddess of harvest. The prestige of Devizes corn market was much enhanced by this provision of a covered area for corn sales, attracting buyers from a wide area and bringing greater custom to the town. It also

The Market Place in the nineteenth century from a painting in the Town Hall.

gave Devizes one of the largest public halls in Wiltshire, which is now adapted to the needs of modern social functions.

Turn now to face the opposite side of the market place.

In the right corner is the Shambles, built of ashlar in 1838 to replace the previous stone hall donated by Henry Addington in 1791. The square clock tower has a clock on each face, and a replica of the original lantern at the entrance was made locally in 1983. Earlier wooden shambles for selling butchers' meat had been situated in the middle of the Market Place or in Wine Street or St John's Street, as this area of Short Street until the late - eighteenth century contained a town gatehouse and an inn called The Black Swan. The present building consists of two consecutive halls, the second on a higher level, with the town coat of arms over the separating arch. It is in use on Tuesdays, Thursdays, Fridays and Saturdays for market stalls. On this side of the Market Place between the Shambles and the present Black Swan Hotel, there were at least twelve inns in the eighteenth century, with their premises and stables running back to the inner town ditch.

Walk now through the car park in the centre of the Market Place to the Fountain.

Walking Tour

Unveiling of the fountain before a crowd of thousands in 1879.

This was erected in 1879 to commemorate Thomas Sotheron Estcourt, who had been MP for Devizes and founded the Wiltshire Friendly Society in 1828. The monument, incorporating a stone octagonal base with a statue, drinking fountain and cattle troughs, was financed entirely by subscription. Its opening in 1879 was a great occasion, with contingents attending from all the Wiltshire Friendly Societies. Shops and houses were decorated with flowers and evergreens and the ceremony was followed by sports in Roundway Park and a dinner at the Corn Exchange.

The Black Swan Hotel (left), decorated for Queen Victoria's Golden Jubilee in 1887.

Cross now to the Corn Exchange side of the Market Place, crossing Station Road and walking past two estate agents' premises, on the site of former inns. Stop by the door of The Pelican to look across at the opposite side of the Market Place.

Ansties' snuff grinding wheel was in use until 1957.

The Ansties' building opposite, on the right hand corner, was reconstructed in 1894 in local red brick from the Devizes brick-works. It housed the headquarters of a tobacco and snuff firm, dating from the eighteenth century, which closed in 1961. Across the intervening Snuff Street (once New Street), with its row of cottages, is the former Co-op building, constructed in 1936 in a modern style which still sits awkwardly in an area of largely Georgian buildings and may soon be demolished. The Black Swan next door, formerly a private house, was re-fronted in 1737 in colour-washed brick. Its courtyard archway formerly led into Devizes cattle market. A little further along stands Parnella House, a stone-fronted eighteenth-century house, the façade adorned with a statue of Aesculapius, the Greek god of healing, proclaiming its former use as the surgery of the Clare family; the present statue is a replacement made in 1960. Both William and his father John Clare were county coroners, John presiding at the Ruth Pierce inquest in 1753.

Continue walking on the same side of the Market Place until you came to No. 16, a seventeenth-century house set back within a courtyard behind eighteenth-century gates surmounted by stone urns.

This was the house of John Kent, Town Clerk, MP and Mayor of Devizes at various times in the early seventeenth century. The west front gable bears the initials J.M.K. for John and his wife Mary, whom he described in his will as 'a most faithful and comfortable yoke-fellow'. An attractive feature of the early eighteenth-century door is the carved shell hood. Next door is one of two Grade I listed houses in Devizes, No. 17, built in the early eighteenth century for lawyer Wadham Locke. A finely proportioned brick house, it has a hipped tile roof, stone window dressings and an adjoining coach house.

John Kent's house in the Market Place.

Now walk from the Market Place towards the northern entrance to the town along Northgate Street, still on the left hand pavement.

On your left are two eighteenth-century buildings which were once inns, now a restaurant and an optician's. Across the road on the right hand pavement are two small shops whose timber structure is overhung with scalloped tiles, one of the few examples remaining in Devizes. Next door to these, set back, is the British School founded in 1822 by the Nonconformist British and Foreign Schools Society. The ground floor is built of ashlar, with the upper floor of Bath stone cut as brick, and the planked door has ornate wrought iron hinges. On your left, visible through an entrance arch to a builder's yard, is the old Northgate Brewery building, part of a long tradition of brewing in the town. Previously it was Robert Waylen's cloth factory. Ahead and dominating this end of the town stands Wadworth's Northgate Brewery, built in 1885 with a gabled centre and with later extensions on both sides. Wadworth's had absorbed many of the smaller breweries in the town and moved to this site, formerly called 'Bell Corner', from the Northgate Brewery that you have just seen. The firm flourishes and is famous both for its 6X beer and for its use of dray horses for local deliveries, re-introduced in 1974, a popular and familiar sight in the town.

> *Continue to walk along this left hand pavement away from the Brewery roundabout.*

On the left, set back from the road, is St Mary's Congregational church, redundant since the amalgamation with St Andrew's Methodist church in 1984 and now an antiques business. The open-air preaching of Rowland Hill, who was pelted with eggs, stones and even three snakes by the Devizes mob, encouraged by the Rector, led to the establishment in 1776 of a simple brick chapel, which is contained within the present ashlar façade erected in the late nineteenth century. Next door is the site of a blacksmith's shop, which, in the eighteenth century, was on the outskirts of the town on the road to Bath. In a few yards, where formerly stood an inn called The Greyhound, we reach Sandcliffe, an early eighteenth-century brick house faced with stone, with contemporary iron ring door handle and cast iron foot scrapers. It was long a doctor's house; a surgery extension is visible on the north side. In the early nineteenth century it was occupied by Dr Brabant, prominent in the reform bill agitation in Devizes in the years 1831-1832. Here the novelist Mary Ann Evans (George Eliot) stayed in 1843 and reputedly had an affair with the doctor.

Next comes a handsome mid-Georgian brick house, with stone Ionic porch, an arched wreathed door fanlight and an eighteenth-century summer house in the grounds. In the days of the landlord William Halcomb, who later moved to The Bear, this was a busy posting inn, the last within the parish boundary, with forty beds, sixty horses and ten post carriages. In 1771, the Earl of Pembroke gave a ball here, attended by the Duke and Duchess of Queensberry, Lady Elizabeth Herbert, Sir Edward Bayntun and

Northgate House, formerly the King's Arms, an eighteenth-century posting inn.

other notables. The inn reverted to private use in the nineteenth century and was subsequently used as Assize Judge's lodgings and Council offices; it now accommodates a firm of solicitors. The stables to the north of the inn later became nursery gardens. The north gate of the town stood just past the north wall of Northgate House.

On the opposite side of the road was The White Lion, built about 1840, whose former name, The Barge, shows that it was patronised by canal workers and bargees. It is now incorporated into the brewery. Next is the Assize Court, designed in Grecian style by T.H. Wyatt in 1835 and financed by subscription to bring trade and prestige to the town. In the late nineteenth century it housed a Government School for Science and Art and in the 1950s served as the police station. At the first appearance of women jurors at the Assizes in 1921 the prisoner in the first case objected and they were replaced by men. This proud building now sits empty awaiting its fate.

> **Still keeping to the left hand side of the road, cross Station Hill.**

Here is the tiny Besborough Lodge, formerly a toll-house on the Bath Road, which then ran along the course of the present canal. It was later used by the lock-keeper, and the Bath stone house opposite was occupied by the Wharfinger. Across the stone Town Bridge, a garage now stands on the site of the former Waggon and Horses inn, a carters' stopping place on the route to Bath.

Cross the busy road by the pedestrian crossing and walk back towards the canal bridge, passing twentieth century flats on your left which replaced the cottages of The Nursery, formerly occupied by nursery gardens. Turn left on to the canal towpath and walk along the canal to the Wharf.

William Dickenson's barge at the canal wharf, c. 1900.

The Kennet and Avon Canal, constructed between 1794 and 1810, linked Bristol and London via these two rivers and facilitated the transport of heavy building materials, coal and agricultural produce by broad barges that could carry up to 60 tons. With the coming of the railway to the west country in 1841, however, the canal fell into decline, and was only rescued in the last fifty years by the Herculean efforts of the Kennet and Avon Canal Trust, which dredged and repaired the waterway and rebuilt locks. Its efforts were crowned with the re-opening of the canal for pleasure boating by the Queen in 1990.

The famous flight of 29 locks on Caen Hill can be visited by walking 1 mile along the towpath in a westerly direction, or by driving along the Bath Road and taking the sign-posted turning on the right to the locks at the bottom of Caen Hill.

As you walk along this short stretch of the canal, you pass the back of Wadworth's Brewery, the canal forge, where horses were shod, and the site of the old gasworks on your right. This section caused great technical problems for the canal engineers because of the porosity of the greensand, which had to be lined with clay from Caen Hill. The wharf originally extended the length of the bank along which you are walking right back to Town Bridge, but part of this ground was bought by the Corporation in 1827 to be used as a gasworks. On the left is one of the pillboxes erected along many inland waterways during the Second World War as a defence against invasion. On the opposite bank is an old warehouse, now converted into a theatre, known as the Wharf Theatre, where there was once a hoist on the upper floor facing the canal and an iron crane to the side.

> ### Cross the curved canal bridge at the end of the towpath.

Like the Town Bridge, this one was made of Limpley Stoke stone for strength. You now approach the Wharf, with its range of warehouses, where formerly there would have been cranes, a weighing engine and coal yards. After the collapse of the Wharf Company in the 1840s, the Council took over the running of the Wharf, and carrier services operated on the canal until the 1920s. Nowadays on Good Fridays, the Wharf is the starting point for the Devizes to Westminster canoe race which, from its small beginning in 1948 as a challenge by a party of Rover Scouts, has blossomed into an international canoeing event. The Wharf warehouses now accommodate the Kennet and Avon Canal Trust visitors' centre,

The first Devizes to Westminster canoe race in 1948.

which is open all the year apart from a short period in the winter; boat trips and walks of the flight of locks leave from here on some Sundays in the summer season.

As you move away from the Wharf area towards the town and walk down Couch Lane, pausing at the Wharfside complex on the left, you are crossing the outer boundary of the town's medieval defences.

The redevelopment of the Wharf in the 1970s with a mixture of residential, craft and specialist shops has transformed a neglected site into an attractive area. Couch Lane is one of the earliest named streets, meaning a lane leading to a cow meadow. As you reach the main road at the end you are faced with a building representing the town's industrial past. On the opposite side of New Park Street stands one of the earliest factories in the west of England, built in 1785 by John Anstie in classical style similar to early factories built in the north and midlands by other pioneers of the Industrial Revolution. Here spinning jennies and weaving looms were used to manufacture 'cassimeres' made from cotton, silk, wool and mohair. After Anstie's bankruptcy in 1793, the building was used for a variety of purposes, including a house of industry for the poor, corn store, corset factory and for militia stores, when it was the scene of a militia riot in 1810. The building has now been converted into residential units. Along Snuff Street opposite can be glimpsed some of the cottages associated with the Anstie family's later tobacco factory.

Turn left into New Park Street

You are now walking along a street parallel to the Market Place, which was formerly known as Back Street and ran in an arc from the north gate to the south gate of the town, between the inner and outer town ditches. In the eighteenth century, many affluent townsmen lived here, but this street has seen much redevelopment since the Second World War, and some historic houses have been lost. On the left, facing John Anstie's cloth factory, at No. 39 stands his house, an eighteenth-century re-building of a fifteenth century cruck house, with a stuccoed front and Doric porch. After passing The Royal Oak, look into the entrance to Nos 44 and 45, which reveals traces of timber-framed houses. At the rear of these

Walking Tour

New Park Street (Back Street) from St Mary's tower, 1900.

The White Hart in New Park Street stood close to what is now Wadworth's car park.

buildings stood a seventeenth-century malthouse, rebuilt in the nineteenth century and in use until 1905.

> *Cross New Park Road, still keeping to the left hand side of the street.*

Brownston House on the left, a Grade I listed house dating from the early eighteenth century, is one of the finest domestic buildings in Devizes, with high quality red rubbed brickwork and limestone window dressings. Through wrought iron gates, the doorway is approached by semi-circular steps, and is surmounted by a segmental pediment with a cupid's head against a pair of folded wings. The house replaced a previous building on the site occupied by Judge Nicholas, one of the judges at the trial of Archbishop Laud in 1641. During early twentieth-century repairs, fragments of an Elizabethan or Jacobean building were discovered. In the nineteenth century, the house was used as a girls' school and more recently as a nurses' home, health authority offices and doctors' surgery. Next door is the coach house.

> **Walk along to the entrance to St Mary's church. This is only open during school hours, with access by the south door.**

The twelfth-century St Mary's church replaced an earlier simpler town church. The chancel dates from the Norman period, with intersecting wall arcading, chevron moulding and quadripartite vaulted roof, but the clerestoried nave, aisles, windows and tower were rebuilt in Perpendicular style in the mid-fifteenth-century period of prosperity in Devizes, by a clothier, William Smyth, whose inscription is on the nave roof- 'Pray for the soul of William Smyth who had this church built and died on 1st June 1436.' The tie beam roof, originally painted in bright colours, rests on corbels representing Henry VI, Queen Margaret and Robert Neville, Bishop of Salisbury between 1427 and 1438. Nineteenth-century alterations revealed traces of floral and biblical paintings on the chancel walls, including the legend of Saint Christopher fording a river, the Assumption of the Blessed Virgin Mary and a turreted castle, but these were painted over at the time of the Reformation.

Traces of wall paintings on interior walls of St Mary's church, from a drawing by Edward Kite.

> **If access cannot be gained to the church, walk round the outside, looking at its exterior features.**

The tower is 91 feet high, the highest tower of all the Devizes churches, and has an embattled parapet, stepped angle buttresses and crocketed pinnacles. A canopied niche on the east exterior gable of the nave contains a late medieval figure of the Virgin Mary, a rare survival from this period; the base of the pedestal features two shields on which are carved William Smyth's initials. Tradition has it that a Cromwellian soldier, trying to pull down the

One of the carved wooden corbels in Great Porch House; Queen Joan of Navarre.

Late medieval statue of the Virgin Mary on roof of St Mary's church.

Transitional Norman south porch, St Mary's church.

statue, fell down and was killed. The south porch is twelfth century Transitional Norman, with chevron moulding and pointed arch. Around the church are grotesques, drip stones and gargoyles, sculptured heads of humans and animals, including a cowled monk, two bears rampant, and a dragon and a man beneath a tree, representing the temptation; the wooden pelican over the south door feeding its young was perhaps originally a roof corbel. Near the south door is a flat tomb, thought to be a dole stone, where loaves were distributed to the poor on Sundays.

> *Return from St Mary's churchyard to New Park Street and walk a few yards left to the Castle Inn.*

The late eighteenth-century Castle Inn, which stands on the site of a former house was built by brewers Charles Rose and John Tylee, of red brick with a mansard roof and sloping corner. It became an important coaching inn, with adjacent stabling for twenty-seven horses and accommodation for a further eighteen horses and four carriages on the opposite side of the road. The first landlord was Thomas Oak, a former corset maker, about whom the following rhyme was written:

> There's little Tommy Oak
> Who looks so very prim,
> He's left off making stays
> To keep the Castle Inn.

> **Cross the link road with care to the black and white house opposite.**

This is one of the two surviving medieval houses in Devizes. Great Porch House was originally a timber-framed three bay hall, open from ground to roof with a two-storey cross wing. The large porch, from which the house took its name, was probably removed from the front of the present passageway when houses were built in the garden court in the seventeenth century. At the same time, an upper floor and central hall chimney were inserted. The fifteenth-century triple Gothic window above the passage, possibly a hall clerestory or chamber window, is rare; the rest of the windows date from the nineteenth century when the house was refaced in brick. The chamfered or furrowed exterior wall and roof beams and the carved barge board point to this being a costly and well finished building. The interior, with its carved heads of Henry IV and Queen Joan of Navarre, and the flower paintings on plaster at each end of the inside of the roof have prompted suggestions that this was the home of a wealthy merchant, such as a member of the Coventry family, or even that it was built for Queen Joan to use while the castle was being repaired.

Cattle fair in Monday Market Street, 1930s. This was the site of early medieval markets.

Walking Tour

Cross the road now to The White Bear.

The Regal cinema, 1950s. The cinema, later used as car showrooms, has now been replaced by Chantry Court flats.

Before the decline of the castle, the earliest market place was outside St Mary's church, then a wide open space before the building of The Castle Inn and the in-filling of Maryport Street. Dating from the sixteenth century, the White Bear, originally called The Talbot, stood in the middle of this open market place. The three gables are Tudor, with original barge boards and finial to the right gable and there are 300 year-old paintings on the beam in the bar. The market cross, which stood at the north-east angle of the inn, was removed about 1615 to the present market place, where it stood for nearly two hundred years. There was also a teasel post here, where teasels were sold to cloth makers for raising the nap on the cloth. In Monday Market Street, which runs in front of and to the side of the inn, were several other inns and in the eighteenth century there was a starch house with stove and hogsties for starch-making and fattening pigs.

Walk now along the pavement in front of the White Bear and turn left into Maryport Street, which consists of seventeenth-, eighteenth- and nineteenth-century in-filling, as the original market place lost its importance.

The clothing shop on the left was formerly an inn called The Saracen's Head and Nos 11, 12 and 13, further along were The

Wholesale grocers, Stratton, Sons and Mead in Monday Market Street, now the site of the Iceland supermarket.

Shoulder of Mutton. The red brick Victorian Gothic building, now a building society office between these former inns, housed the National Society girls' school in 1881 and later became The Oddfellows' Hall.

On the opposite side of the street stands The Three Crowns. Originally a late-sixteenth-century and early-seventeenth-century building, it was altered in the nineteenth century but retains its Jacobean gables with ornamented barge boards and cast iron gutter across the foot of the gables. The inn, in the possession of the Phipp family for nearly a century, brewed its own beer and specialized in old French brandy. One of the earliest inns to have electric light, generated by its own plant, it was also a posting house and supplied coal to the barracks and the asylum, having warehouses and stables in New Park Street. For the coronation celebrations in 1911, the premises were adorned with 6,000 blooms, with the four upstairs rooms decorated as spring, summer, autumn and winter. Inside is a model of the decorated pub.

At the end of Maryport Street bear left into Sidmouth Street, named after Viscount Sidmouth, the town's MP for many years. Pause by the entrance to the supermarket.

Here stood the hospital of St John the Baptist founded by 1314, but dissolved in 1548, although the chapel survived as late as 1666 and

Walking Tour

The Three Crowns in Maryport Street, decorated for the coronation of George V in 1911.

gave the name Chapel Corner Street to this part of the town, which later became Leg o' Mutton Street after a pub half way along, and finally Sidmouth Street. On the opposite side of the road is Handel House, a three-storey Bath stone building on the site of a timber yard and near the horse pond. Formerly a draper's warehouse, it was used as Assize Judge's lodgings prior to 1868 and became a music shop at the turn of the century, as the wall plaques below the roof with the names of Mendelssohn, Bach, Handel, Mozart and Beethoven, reveal. It remained a music shop for almost a century in the ownership of the Price family of Bournemouth and is now a bookshop and art gallery. Next to it is Albion Place, dating from the late eighteenth and early

'Wiltshire's Corner', now the site of Sainsbury's supermarket.

nineteenth centuries and embellished with a cast iron balcony porch and stone verandah. About two thirds of the way along Sidmouth Street stood the eastern gate of the town on the line of the outer ditch.

> *Cross now towards Handel House and turn into Sheep Street, which rejoins the semi-circular street pattern between the north and south gates, walking on the left hand pavement.*

Behind Handel House stands a seventeenth-century timber-framed house, re-fronted in the eighteenth century in red and blue brick and now a restaurant; this was The Angel Inn, from which the street formerly took its name and which in the days of the Handel House music shop was a workshop for repairing and making musical instruments. A little further on is the Baptist chapel, built in the mid-nineteenth century of Chilmark stone in Early English style, near the site of a former Presbyterian meeting house and before that an inn called The Sampson. The rest of the street is occupied by two- and multi-storey council flats, built during the post-war slum clearance of a densely populated area consisting of small cottages and thirteen courts of houses.

> *At the end of Sheep Street, look left up Hare and Hounds Street, formerly Kilberry Row.*

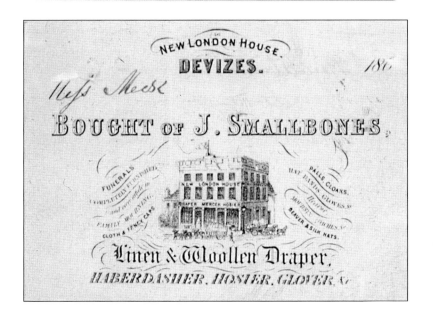

Bill head of draper James Smallbones, who occupied the present Handel House in the nineteenth century.

Half way along, the outer town ditch crosses the street, and passes behind the houses in Bridewell Street. The Hare and Hounds pub was also a brewery in the late nineteenth century and early twentieth century. At the top end of Hare and Hounds Street is the Green, purchased by the Council in 1899 as a public recreation area.

> *If desired, the walk can be extended at this point, crossing the large Green over Southbroom Road, passing Southbroom House, now Devizes School, and continuing to the small Green across Nursteed Road, towards St James's church and the Crammer pond.*

The name Crammer probably comes from the German word 'kramer' meaning tradesman. This area, formerly part of the wasteland of Bishops Cannings manor, was used for fairs and stalls, and the pond is also the supposed site of the Moonraker legend, in which canny Wiltshire smugglers duped the excisemen by hiding their kegs of brandy in the pond and pretending to be raking for 'the gurt big cheese', the reflection of the moon, when challenged.

> *With or without this detour, proceed now from the corner of Sheep Street across the road into Bridewell Street.*

Skating on the frozen Crammer, 1960s.

St James's, or 'the Green church'.

The houses on your left are part of an imaginative development of run down property in the 1980s, emphasising variety of colour and shape and refurbishment rather than demolition, in stark contrast to the harsh outlines of the Sheep Street flats that you passed earlier.

Stop opposite a passageway with L M 1906 on the keystone.

To the left of the archway and Archway House, is a mid-eighteenth-century building formerly The Curriers Arms, and later The Duke of Wellington. The wide door enabled horses to be brought through the passage to stables at the back. Here in 1848 local farmers armed with bludgeons laid siege to Chartists from Trowbridge and Bath, who were attempting to hold political meetings in the town. This plot of ground has been occupied since medieval times and after the pub closed in 1866 it became a builder's shop, with a lime pit and woodworking machines at the rear. A little further along on the same side is the site of the old Bridewell, the first Wiltshire county prison set up in 1579 and still retaining a Queen Anne door, with its original nails, iron grating and heavy knocker. John Howard in his report on The State of the Prisons in 1788 revealed that a prisoner, Thomas Platt, had died here in solitary confinement through hunger and cold. After the new prison was built on the Bath Road in 1810, the Bridewell was used for prisoners awaiting trial; later it became a police station, a crèche and a nurse's home. It now provides sheltered housing.

Walking Tour

Continue to walk along the left hand pavement of Bridewell Street.

The present ambulance station is on the site of the Figgins and Gent Brewery, established in the second half of the eighteenth century and before that a religious house stood there, owned by the Knights Hospitallers; a map of 1737 refers to Bridewell Street as Friar Street.

At the end of Bridewell Street, turn left into Long Street, walking up to the last house on the left, almost opposite Hillworth Road.

This house is now the Conservative Club, but was originally the home of Robert Sutton, of the clothier family. In the nineteenth century it became Wilsford House School, with grounds, including a tennis court and cricket pitch, extending to Southbroom Road and Bridewell Street. Opposite the end of the garden wall is the entrance to Hillworth Road, site of the south gate of Devizes; from here onwards, Long Street became Townend. The first part of Hillworth Road runs along the outer town ditch, formerly known as Gallows Ditch because it led to the town gallows and to Hartmoor Road, the old road to Potterne and Lavington. The present Potterne Road leading south out of town dates only from 1750.

Cross the road to the entrance of Hillworth Road. If time allows, the walk can be extended to include a visit to Hillworth Park; the entrance is in Hillworth Road on the left hand side, just past Hillworth Gardens on the opposite side.

On the left is Mirehouse, in the turret room of which the Devizes troop of Boy Scouts was formed in 1908, one of the first in the country.

The park, with some fine mature trees and formal gardens, lies behind the early-nineteenth century Hillworth House and contains an eighteenth-century summer house and a seventeenth-century Quaker burial garden.

From the entrance to Hillwoth Road walk down Long Street back towards the town centre.

PLEASE COMPLETE IN BLOCK CAPITALS:

NAME *B. M. Theo*
MR & MRS Thompson

ADDRESS 51 Highheads
Poltrene

Tel No 01380 720 616 .... Postcode

E-mail ....

Can we put you on our mailing list? ☑

Wiltshire Heritage Museum, 41 Long Street, Devizes, SN10 1NS. 01380 727369
www.wiltshireheritage.org.uk

EXPLORE | IMAGINE | DISCOVER

WILTSHIRE HERITAGE MUSEUM

Interested in helping us preserve our wonderful collections?

Then join the Wiltshire Archaeological and Natural History Society

Fill in your details on the reverse of this card and we will send you more information.

WILTSHIRE
HERITAGE
MUSEUM
DEVIZES

There is a splendid vista of high quality eighteenth-century brick and stucco-fronted houses, with the sash windows, Doric porches and pedimented doorways typical of eighteenth-century domestic architecture. These houses were built or rebuilt by wealthy clothiers or professional men. Stone was still expensive, so it was used sparingly for window and door dressings or just for façades and high status houses. Local brick earth, however, was readily available, and the brick industry grew rapidly in the town with the discovery of Gault clay at the bottom of Caen Hill during the construction of the canal. Some sixteen houses in Long Street along which you are walking were private schools in the eighteenth and nineteenth centuries, such as Verecroft and the Revd Fenner's school at No. 40. This school had a fives court ('3s 6d extra') and the boys were fed on liver, cabbage, rice and figgy puddings. No. 39, the Rectory, was purchased in 1776 with Queen Anne's Bounty. Previously a Rectory stood on the site of the present parish room further along and was described in 1783 as 'a small thatched cottage' with a strip of glebe land. Wiltshire Archaeological and Natural History Society, with its museum and library, is housed in Nos 40 and 41 Long Street, which in earlier times have been a doctor's house and a school. The Gothic entrance and oriel type bay window were inserted into the eighteenth-century façade in 1874 when the Society moved here from other premises. The museum is well worth a visit for its outstanding collection of prehistoric artefacts and the interesting local and natural history galleries, as well as its library.

Many of the houses on the east side of Long Street conceal earlier timber-framed structures, which were re-fronted in the eighteenth century with plaster and stucco, or brick with stone dressings. Nos 15 and 16 still show their over-sailing first floors. From Morris Lane onwards, there are some fine individual houses, such as Lansdowne House with its white stuccoed front, and No. 10 in red brick with stone window dressings. No. 9 with a late eighteenth-century front to a sixteenth-century timber frame, is in Bath stone, with an arched yard entrance and mews buildings. Its neighbour, No. 8, in brick and stone, was the house of Joseph Needham, a surgeon; it has ornamental vases surmounting the parapet of the street frontage and a projecting shell hood over the door. Originally, like Parnella House, it had a statue of Aesculapius in a niche, now bricked up. At the end of Long Street on the right is The Elm Tree inn, so named from the large elm that used to grow in front. It was formerly called

The Salutation, and has a Jacobean timber structure and over-sailing first floor.

At the foot of Long Street is the Jacobean-style building erected in 1848 for the Wiltshire Friendly Society. The Black Horse formerly stood here, with its own brewery and stabling for sixty horses. Opposite on the right in High Street, an imposing façade of Bath stone fronts Prince Sutton's brick house, built on his marriage in 1731; the original rainwater head survives on the left hand side.

> **Turn left at the bottom of Long Street into St John's Street, sometimes called Church Street, which starts behind the Town Hall.**

The earlier preoccupation of the town with the cloth trade is illustrated in the former name of The Lamb, The Scribbling Horse, from the frame on which cloth was stretched for scribbling or cleaning. It is likely that the front of this inn was refurbished with waste materials when the old Wool Hall opposite was being demolished in the early nineteenth-century to make way for the new town hall. During the civil war, Roundhead soldiers were billeted there and James Wolfe later stayed in the back part of the inn on a recruiting drive before leaving to fight the French in Canada. Next to The Lamb, a single-storey, cruck house was altered in the seventeenth and eighteenth centuries and became three storeys; the year 1740 carved on the rainwater head marks its refurbishment rather than its original construction.

> **Turn left now into St John's Court.**

Nos 1 to 3 on the left were probably built as one unit, oak-framed and jettied and dating from around 1590-1600; they were stuccoed and given sash windows in the eighteenth century. The wall of No. 1 exposes round timber pegs and carpenters' marks as well as the earliest herringbone brickwork in Devizes. The kitchen of this house contains a 10ft-wide stone arch with chevron moulding, perhaps obtained when the castle was being demolished in the seventeenth century. The inner shell of No. 4, St John's Court on the opposite side is one of the oldest houses in Devizes, built for a Mayor, Thomas Coventry, who died in 1451. The Coventry family were benefactors of the town, Thomas leaving rents to pay for the upkeep of almshouses and his brother William providing lead for the roof of St Mary's church. Originally a timber-framed hall open to the roof, with smoke-blackened timbers, it was partly converted to stone in the sixteenth century, the earliest example of domestic stone building in Devizes and was later completely re-fronted in the nineteenth century.

> *Proceed now towards St John's church and pass through the gate, taking the left hand path along a brick wall, pausing at the last house on the left.*

Rainwater head, dated 1733, on Chancel End.

This house is called Chancel End and has the date 1733 on its rainwater head. The house turns forty-eight degrees with the line of the churchyard path.

St John's church, originally within the outer bailey of the castle, is slightly later than St Mary's church and contains even finer examples of Norman work. The tower is Norman, embellished with intersecting arcading and semi-circular headed windows. The fourth angle of the tower has an embattled turret, originally with a small spire. The east end of the church is flanked by the Lamb and Beauchamp chapels, of elaborate fifteenth-century Perpendicular style with battlements and Tudor carving. There is also a reminder of the Civil War in the wall of the Beauchamp chapel. Shot holes are still visible from a bombardment by Parliamentarian forces during the siege of Devizes in 1643.

> *Walk now along the path on the south side of the church to the south porch which normally is open.*

St John's church.

On the south transept, two Norman semi-circular-headed windows have been blocked up to make way for a fifteenth-century Perpendicular window. Notice also on this side a mass clock high up on the wall, and the grotesques supporting the water courses.

> *Inside the church, move to the centre aisle and face the east end.*

Green man carving on a capital in the choir of St John's church.

The chancel, approached through three Norman arches with scalloped and foliated capitals, has interlaced arches with chevron moulding and fish scale work, originally coloured, and stars painted on the rib-vaulted groined roof. A Green Man can be seen peeping from one of the capitals in the choir. Only the window to the left of the altar on the north side is original Norman; the others were restored in the Norman style in the nineteenth century. As the tower is rectangular, not square, it is supported on two semi-circular and two pointed arches, perhaps the earliest examples of the pointed arch in England. Until the insertion of a ringing floor in the fifteenth century, the tower would have been open to the roof, with interlaced triple arcading visible from below. The nave was reconstructed with pointed arches in Perpendicular style in the fifteenth century and aisles and porches were added; a generation later the Lamb and Beauchamp chapels were built, with richly carved oak roof panelling. The Beauchamp chapel incorporates some grotesques, originally on the exterior of the building. Monuments within the church commemorate some of the town's great families, such as the Suttons, Estcourts and Heathcotes.

Leave the church by the south porch, turn right and walk to the west end.

Grotesque in the Beauchamp chapel in St John's church.

A 15ft high listed obelisk is visible in the churchyard that records a 1751 fatality when a party of five were drowned while boating on a Sunday on Drew's Pond. The monument was financed by public subscription as 'a solemn Monitor to Young People to Remember their Creator in the days of their youth' and the inscription reads 'Remember the Sabbath to keep it holy'. Nearby to your right is a gabled almshouse of 1615, rebuilt in stone on an earlier timber frame. The ground and first floors each contained two rooms for poor widows of the two parishes and the two basement rooms were used for the paupers of St John' parish. The inmates were expected to be regular churchgoers and were fined for offences such as brawling or not keeping their rooms clean. The rules were read aloud to them once a quarter.

An optional small detour, not possible in a wheelchair, can be made over an old railway bridge from which the disused railway tunnel (obscured by trees in summer) and the top of the Victorian castle are visible on the right.

From a position a little way along Estcourt Hill, you can get an idea of the massive size of the dry valley below the castle. From the top of Estcourt Hill, where it meets Hillworth Road, there is a good view over the town, from the point where the town gallows is believed to have stood.

Proceed now back through the churchyard toward the gate by which you entered the churchyard, passing a seventeenth-century black and white cottage and nineteenth-century cottages in Tudor style and turning left back through St John's Court towards St John's Street.

This narrow street was not widely used as a thoroughfare until the 1825 Improvement Commission removed jutting out buildings, the High Street being more easily accessible. The brick houses here are mostly eighteenth-century, many on earlier timber frames and some were inns, such as the original Pelican, by the arched entrance to Castle Court, and The Woolpack, now a house. The white building with the Doric porch was originally The Red Lion.

Just past this building, stop and look back at The Town Hall.

This was built in the years 1806-1808, replacing the seventeenth-century Wool Hall and the Tudor Yarn Hall. It provides the focal point in St John's Street and was one of the few Bath stone buildings in the town before the opening of the Kennet and Avon canal in 1810. Of an elegant and symmetrical design, it has a graceful curved facade and a row of Ionic columns and the heads of its cast lead rainwater pipes are decorated with the town coat of arms. A 24-pound Sebastopol gun, presented to the town in 1857 by the Secretary of War, was moved to the front of the hall here from its first position in the Market Place, but was removed for salvage in the Second World War.

Cross the road now towards the tea-rooms and proceed into St John's Alley, which is sign-posted.

Walking Tour

The Sebastopol gun outside the Town Hall, presented to Devizes in 1857 and scrapped during the Second World War.

The Tanners' market was held on the corner close to where the tea-rooms now stand. St John's Alley is a street of recently restored sixteenth- and seventeenth-century timber-framed houses with brick and plaster in-filling and jettied first floors with curved beam ends. The oak timber came from nearby Melksham Forest and was fixed with wooden pegs not nails. The first building on the left has a long history as an inn, called at various times The Hart, The Boot and The Wheatsheaf. The house on the left at the end of the alley has been tree-ring dated to 1646 and evidently was the home and workplace of a substantial merchant. The cottages on the opposite side are later in-fill. This cobbled alley was originally broader and led through into Wine Street, but when St John's Street was widened in the early-nineteenth century, it became a pedestrian alley and this perhaps has safeguarded it from unsympathetic development.

Leave the alley and turn to the right, proceeding along St John's Street on the right-hand pavement.

On the opposite side of the road is a chequered red and blue early-eighteenth century house, later used as both post office and police station. Through the access road next to it can be glimpsed the castle gatehouse, dating from 1860, leading to the Victorian castle built on the site of the medieval fortress, of which almost nothing now remains. This modern, neo-Gothic castle was built by Devizes businessman Valentine Leach and his son between 1840 and 1880. It is now privately owned and not accessible to the public.

Continue to the next corner and look back across the road.

St John's Alley from a
watercolour by Margaret
Ewart, 1895.

This was formerly The Crown Inn, in continuous use from 1544 to
1966 and much used in the coaching era. It was advertised in 1869
as having stables for forty horses. On the opposite corner, at the
angle of Wine Street, is the old Boots building of 1912, now
occupied by a bank and a building society. Its carved heads set in
circular wall plaques commemorate famous figures in the town's
history, Roger Bishop of Salisbury, Matilda, Hubert de Burgh,
Edward I, Sir Ralph Hopton and Thomas Lawrence.

**Cross the road towards the opposite corner and then
turn to look back at the Old Town Hall.**

This was erected in 1752 on the site of the Guildhall, which was
pulled down in 1750. Part of the Bath stone façade came from a
mansion in Bowden Park and the ground floor was originally open
to the street to accommodate the cheese market and fish stalls as
late as 1832. From 1836 until 1956 it housed a wine business,
which gave the street its name. Brick- and stone-arched cellars
stretched under the road, and William Cunnington's customers

included Buckingham Palace and the British Embassy in St Petersburg. In 1878 Alfred Cunnington assembled the first telephone in commercial use to connect the wine business here with his home at Southgate House. One Long Street resident refused to allow the line to pass above his house for fear that it would attract lightning. The building was later used as militia stores, mess rooms for the Devizes Volunteers and a laundry. Fortunately a proposal in 1939 to demolish it to make way for a modern flat-roofed shop was not pursued.

> *Now proceed along Wine Steet towards the Brittox, site of the stockaded pathway that once led towards the medieval castle.*

Boots Corner, with commemorative wall plaques and a copper dome, was built in 1912.

On the left side of Wine Street was the Weavers Hall, used for meetings of the Drapers Company until 1769. On the opposite side of the Little Brittox, the George or Antelope provided them with liquid refreshment. By the junction of High Street and Wine Street stood the Butter Cross.

> *Turn left now into the Little Brittox and walk back towards the Market Place.*

Williams' beer shop in the Little Brittox, c. 1900. This shop is now Terry's the chemists.

The fishmonger and greengrocer's shop on the right-hand side is the site of The Bull's Head patronised by shearmen and cloth workers in the town. A little further on the right is the opening to what used to be Mortimer's Court, named after an eighteenth-century baker who made the famous Devizes simnel cakes. This area and the adjacent Shambles were part of an entrance to the castle's outer defences from Short Street where there was a gatehouse.

And so we return to the Market Place, where we began. Inevitably many places of interest have been omitted, but we have walked along the same streets that our medieval predecessors knew and seen some tangible reminders of Devizes' colourful history over 900 years.

The Next Steps

Readers who wish to pursue further their interest in Devizes history should visit two museums in Devizes.

Wiltshire Heritage Museum at 41, Long Street, houses an internationally renowned collection of prehistoric artefacts. Other galleries cover Roman, Saxon and medieval archaeology, as well as natural history and geology. The Local History gallery contains exhibits illustrating the modern history of Devizes and district. The Museum is open from Monday to Saturday from 10 a.m. to 5 p.m.

The Kennet and Avon Canal Museum, housed in a former granary at the canal Wharf, is open daily from 10 a.m. to 4.30 p.m., apart from certain weeks in the winter. Walks along the canal flight of locks start from here on Sunday afternoons in summer and short boat trips leave from the Wharf on Sunday mornings and afternoons.

Further information on seasonal events and exhibitions in the town can be obtained from Devizes Visitor Centre in the Market Place.

Anyone wishing to carry out detailed research on the history of Devizes should visit the following libraries:-

Wiltshire Archaeological and Natural History Society Library, at 41, Long Street, which contains extensive manuscript, printed and pictorial material relating to Devizes and a unique collection of indexed newspaper cuttings dating back to 1750, as well as all the bound copies of *The Devizes Gazette*.

The Local Studies Library at Bythesea Road in Trowbridge has collections of newspapers, printed material and photographs and is open from 9 30 a.m. to 5.p.m. from Monday to Friday.

The Wiltshire Record Office, also in Bythesea Road in Trowbridge, holds archival material such as deeds, wills and borough records and is open from 9.30 a.m. to 5 p.m. from Monday to Friday.

Among the most useful published sources of information for the history of Devizes are the following:

Barron, R.S., *The Geology of Wiltshire* (1976)
Bradby, E., *The Book of Devizes* (1985)
Bray, N., *A Wiltshire Railway Remembered* (1984)
Burne, A.H., *More Battlefields of England* (1952)
Buxton, D. and Girvan, J., *A Devizes Camera* (1983)
Buxton, D. and Girvan, J., *A Devizes Camera II* (1986)
Buxton, D., *Around Devizes in Old Photographs* (1990)
Buxton, D., *Devizes Voices* (1996)
Clew, K.R., *The Kennet and Avon Canal* (1968)
Clifton-Taylor, A., *Another Six English Towns* (1984)
Colman, P., *Devizes in Old Picture Postcards* (1983)
Cunnington, B.H., *Some Annals of the Borough of Devizes*,
    (2 *vols.*1925-6)
D.o E. *List of Buildings of Special Architectural or Historic Interest;*
    the Borough of Devizes (1972)
Girvan, J., *Devizes in Focus* (1989)
Haycock, L., *John Anstie of Devizes, an Eighteenth-Century*
    Wiltshire Clothier (1991)
Haycock, L., *Devizes in the Civil War* (2000)
Haycock, L. (ed.), *A Devizes Century* (1999)
Kite, E., *The Bear Inn;* WAS Library; W.T.114
Kite, E., *The Churches of Devizes;* W.A.M. 2, 1855
Pevsner, N., *Wiltshire* (1963)
Piper, J., *Topographical Letter from Devizes;*
    Cornhill Magazine, Nov. 1944
Potter, K. (ed), *Gesta Stephani* (1955)
Stone, E.H., *Devizes Castle* (1920)
The Victoria History of the Counties of England; Wiltshire,
    vols.4, 5 and 10
Waylen, J., *Chronicles of the Devizes* (1839)
Waylen, E. & J., *Nonconformity in Devizes;*
    bound cuttings from *The Devizes Advertiser* (1877)
Waylen, J., *A History, Military and Municipal of the*
    Ancient Borough of The Devizes (1859)
Waylen, J., *Wiltshire during the Civil Wars;*
    bound cuttings from *The Wiltshire Independent* (1840)
Wicks, A., *Bellum Civile; Sir Ralph Hopton's Memoirs*
    of the Campaign in the West 1642-1644 (1988)

Index

Addington, Henry, 1st Viscount Sidmouth   53, 67, 94, 95
Adlam, Samuel   51
Albion Place   110
Anne, Edward   32
Anstie, Benjamin   68
Anstie, Benjamin Webb   46
Anstie, John, senior   46
Anstie, John, junior   45, 52, 103
Anstie, Paul   68
Anstie's cloth factory   45, 103
Ansties' tobacco factory   64, 66, 70, 86, 87, 97
Assize Court   75, 85, 100
Asylum   70, 77

Baldwin, Thomas   54
Baptists   41, 56, 57, 111
Barford House   51
Bassett, Philip   19
Baster, Joseph   46
Bath Road   17, 60, 66
Batt, Richard   31
Bayntun, Edward   35
Bayntun, Revd Henry   51
Bear Club, The   55
Bear Hotel, The   13, 52, 58, 61, 62, 73, 74, 80, 93, 94, 99
Beauchamp Chapel   25, 36, 117, 118
Bennett, Richard   32
Bent, John   34
Berks & Hants Extension Railway   8, 72
Bevan, John   48
Black Horse, The   116
Black Swan, The   51, 59, 97
Book of Constitutions, The   26, 27
Boot, The   120
Boulter, Thomas   62
Brabant, Dr R.H.   68, 99
Bradford-on-Avon   45, 46
Bridewell, The   33, 54, 65, 113
Bridewell Street   33, 46, 112, 113
Brickley Lane   60, 88
Bristol   38, 39
British School, The   69, 98
Brittox, The   13, 22, 35, 56, 65, 70, 91, 122

Broadleas   88
Bromham House   41
Brown & May   70, 85, 87
Browne, Thomas   49
Brownston House   49, 104, 105
Bull's Head, The   122
Burgh, Hubert de   15, 16
Burney, Fanny   61
Burrough, James   46
Byron, John, Sir   37

Caen Hill   63, 101, 102, 115
Caen Hill brickworks   64, 70
Caen Hill locks   62, 63, 101
Cannings   8, 10, 39
carriers   59, 73, 80
Castle Inn, The   58, 67, 106
Castle Lane   13
Central Wilts Bacon Company   83, 87
Chancel End   117
Chapel Corner   33, 110
Charles I   35, 39, 41
Charles II   42
Charlotte, Queen   55
Chartists   113
Chequers, The   58
Chippenham   36
Chippenham Forest   15
Chivers   81, 85, 86
Chivers, William Edward   85
Clare family   50, 97
Coleman, Philip   31, 32
Commercial Road   18
Congregational chapel   57, 99
Congregationalists   57
Conscience Lane   46
Co-op, The   83, 97
Corn Exchange, The   13, 62, 74, 75, 94, 96
Corporation/ Common Council, The   26, 28, 33, 41, 42, 67, 68
Couch Lane   64, 103
County House of Correction, The   41
Coventry, Thomas   23, 117
Coventry, William   22, 117
Crammer, The   41, 88, 90, 91, 112

Cromwell, Oliver   39
Cross Keys Yard   58
Cross Manufacturing   84
Crown, The   58, 73, 121
Cunnington, Alfred   79, 122
Cunnington, William   121
Curriers Arms, The   113

Davis, Dr James   7
Devizes Advertiser, The   69
Devizes Bank   48
Devizes Castle   10, 12-16, 36, 40, 72, 120
Devizes Hospital   79
Devizes Prison   65, 66
Devizes Station   71, 72, 82
Devizes Theatre, The   55
Devizes & Westminster Canoe Race   102
Devizes & Wiltshire Gazette   68
Dore, Edward   45, 46
Drew's Pond   118
Dunkirk Hill   46, 60, 63

Edney, James   59
Edward I   16-18
Edward III   19
Edward VI   34
Eliot, George   99
Elizabeth I   34, 41
Elizabeth II   101
Elm Tree, The   58, 116
Estcourt, Thomas   55
Estcourt, Thomas Sotheron   75, 96
Estcourt Street   70, 71, 85
Estcroft Hill   17, 119
Etchilhampton   7, 60
Etchilhampton Hill   60, 74
Eyles, Edward   52
Eyles, John   42

Fenner, Revd   115
Figgins, Matthew   31
Figgins & Gent   46, 114
Fitzhubert, Robert   14
Five Lanes   17
flax factory   84, 85
Fountain, The   75, 96
Franklin, Richard Bundy   42, 43

Gaigers   70, 86
Gains Lane   22
Gallows Ditch   13, 56, 114
Garrick, David   61
gasworks   102
Geoffrey, Count of Anjou   14
George III   55, 62

Gibbon, Edward   55
Gillman, Charles   69
Gloucester   15, 39
Grange, The   33
Great Porch House   22, 90, 107
Great Western Railway   64
Green, The   8, 33, 55, 58, 60, 68, 74, 88, 91, 112
Greystone House   51
Guildhall, The   28, 29, 54, 121

Halcomb, William   62, 99
Hampton's Dairy   82
Handel House   110
Hare & Hounds, The   112
Hare & Hounds Street   90, 112
Harman, Richard   32
Hartmoor   17, 60
Hartmoor Road   17, 114
Hazelrigg, Sir Arthur   37
Henry I   10, 14
Henry II   15
Henry III   15-18
Henry VII   21
Henry VIII   31
Hertford, Marquis of   36
Hervey, Count of Brittany   14, 15
High Street   29, 116
Hill, Rowland   57, 99
Hillman, Stephen   44
Hillworth House   114
Hillworth Park   56, 90
Hillworth Road   13, 33, 114
Hinchley's   87
Hopton, Ralph, Sir   35-37
Hospital of St John the Baptist   109
Humfrey, Rowland   40
Hunt, Henry, 'Orator'   67

Improvement Commission 1780   48
Improvement Commission 1825   65, 119
inns – see named inns and chapter 7
International Stores   83
Isabella, Queen   15

James I   28, 41
James II   42
John, King   15, 17
Jump Farm   82
Jump Hill   36

Kennet & Avon Canal   49, 62-64, 94, 101, 119
Kennet District Council   91
Kent, John   26, 29, 97
King's Arms, The   99, 100
Knights Hospitallers   114

Lamb, The   52, 54, 116
Lamb chapel, The   25, 117, 118
Lansdowne, battle of, 1643   35
Lansdowne House   51, 115
Lavington   8
Lawrence, Thomas, senior   61, 62
Lawrence, Thomas, junior, RA   61, 94
Leach, Robert Valentine   77
Leach, Valentine   77, 120
Leach, William   46, 48
Leland, John   12, 27, 31, 93
Le Marchant Barracks   77
Literary & Scientific Institute, The   69
Little Brittox, The   82, 122
Lloyd, Sir Charles   39-41
Locke, Wadham   50, 68, 97
Long, James   60
Long Street   22, 46, 50, 51, 58, 115
Lower Park Farm   17
Lydeway   60

Malmesbury Abbey   24
Margaret of France   16
Marlborough Downs   7
Mary I   34, 41
The Market Cross   54, 93
Market Lavington   19
Market Place   18, 22, 93
Maryport Street   18, 57, 81, 108
Maslen's   86
Matilda, Queen   14, 15
Matilda of Ramsbury   14
Mayenne Place   88
Measuring House, The   29
Mechanics' Institute, The   69
Melksham Forest   15, 120
Merchant Guild, The   19, 29
Merewether, Francis   49
Monday Market Street   18, 22, 55, 60, 82, 88, 103
Morris, Grave   32
Morris, Henry   31
Morris Lane   31, 33, 36, 37
Mortimer's Court   122
Mother Anthony's Well   7
Municipal Corporations Act 1835   27, 68

National School, The   69, 109
Needham, Joseph   51, 115
Needham Taylor, Captain   79
New Hall, The   54, 121
New Port, The   21, 22, 58
New Street (Snuff Street)   22, 97, 103
New Park   15, 17, 52-54
New Park Street   18, 22, 45, 52, 60, 82, 88, 103
Nicholas, Robert   35

Norden, John   12
Northgate Brewery   70, 99
Northgate House   52, 75, 91, 100
Northgate Street   22, 46, 57, 64, 69, 75
North Wilts Dairy   84, 87
Nursery, The   88, 101
Nursteed   60
Nursteed Road   8

Oak, Thomas   106
The Oddfellows Hall   81, 109
Offer's   86
Old Park   7, 15, 17, 20
Old Port, The   21, 22, 58
Old Sarum   10
Old Swan Yard   32, 58
Osmund, Bishop of Salisbury   10, 12
Oxford   14, 35-37, 39

Page, William   20
Palace Cinema, The   81
Pans Lane   7, 8, 70
Parnella House   50, 97, 116
Pelican, The   61, 94
Penates   8
Pewsey Vale   6, 7, 72, 74, 91
Pierce, Richard   35, 36, 41
Pierce, Ruth   48, 54, 94, 97
Police   65
Potterne   8, 10, 17, 39
Pugh's Grammar School   69

Quakers   56
Quaker burial ground   115
Quakers' Walk   17, 61

radio station   82
Read, Richard   48
Rectory, The   50, 115
Red House, The   52
Reform Act, First, 1832   68
Reform Act, Second   68
Rendell, William   85
Rennie, John   63
Robert, Duke of Normandy   10
Roches, Peter des, Bishop of Winchester   15
Rochester Castle   12
Roger Bishop of Salisbury   10, 12, 14, 17
Rokell, Richard de   19
Rose and Tylee   46, 106
Rose's butchers   82
Roundway Down   7, 8, 38
Roundway Down, battle of, 1643   37-39
Roundway Hill   37, 79, 81
Roundway Hospital   8, 70, 77

Roundway House   52
Roundway Park   17
Rowde   10, 15, 38, 39

Sandcliffe   52, 99
Savages   87
Scribbling Horse, The   58
Sebastopol gun, The   119, 120
Shambles, The   28, 29, 40, 54, 65, 79, 95, 122
Shane's Castle   60
Sheep Street   33, 57, 88, 111
Sheep Street courts   88, 89
Short Street   13, 28, 122
Sidmouth Street   54, 65, 110, 111
Simnel cakes   26, 122
Simpson, George   68
Sloper, Charles   80, 83
Sloper, Marler   83, 84
Smith, Joshua   55
Smyth, William   20, 25, 105
Somerset & Weymouth Railway   72
Southbroom   7, 8, 90
Southbroom House   41, 52, 112
Southgate House   79, 122
Station Road   22, 33, 79
St James' Church   36, 60
St John's Alley   19, 23, 65, 120
St John's Church   16, 23-25, 36, 41, 43, 46, 117, 118
St John's Court   23, 116, 117
St John's Street   29, 54, 119, 120
St Mary's Church   18, 20, 23-26, 42, 58, 105, 106,
   108
Stephen of Blois   14, 15
Strachey, John   40
Stratton's   87
Stukeley, William   8, 40
Sunnyside Farm   17
Sutton family   44
Sutton, James   48, 52, 53
Sutton, Prince   51
Sutton, Robert   51, 114

Tan Hill Fair   79, 80
Three Crowns, The   109
Thurnam, Dr John   77

Tidcombe, Michael   41
Town Hall   29, 33, 54, 55, 119
Trowbridge   46
Trust for Devizes, The   90
Turnpike gates   73
Turnpike Trusts   60
Tylee, John   64

Vyze blankets   20

Wadworth, Henry   70
Wadworth's Brewery   46. 70, 99, 101
Waiblingen Way   88
Walker, Peter   45
Waller, Sir William   35-38
Warwick, Earl of   19, 58
Waylen, Robert   45, 68, 70, 99
Wayside Farm   8
Weavers Hall, The   29, 122
Wesley, Charles   57
Wesley, John   57
Wharf, The   90, 64, 102
Wharf Theatre   102
Whatley, George   61
Whistley   17
White, T.H.   70, 85
White Bear, The   18, 58, 108
Wick   7
Wick Lane   60
Wiltshire Archaeological and Natural
   History Society   27, 115
Wiltshire Friendly Society   75, 96, 116
Wiltshire Independent, The   69
Wiltshire Regiment, The   77
Wiltshire Times, The   69
Wine Street   23, 28, 29, 54, 65
Wine Street Alley   23
Wolfe, General James   116
Wool Hall, The   29, 33, 42, 54, 116, 119
Wyatt, Benjamin   94
Wyatt, James   52-54
Wyatt, T.H.   70, 75, 77, 100

Yarn Hall, The   29, 119